Rarely has any writer addressed the issue of values in psychotherapy as cogently and comprehensively as has Robert Woolfolk in this groundbreaking volume. This book should be read by the providers and consumers of psychotherapy as well as by anyone with an intellectual interest in the current status of this important form of treatment.

—*Aaron T. Beck, M.D.*
University Professor
Emeritus
University of Pennsylvania
School of Medicine
Department of Psychiatry

The Cure of Souls is a philosophic analysis of some of the most important aspects of psychotherapy that are often neglected by practicing therapists. To understand what some of the basic issues of psychotherapy are and how it can be made more practical and scientific, this book is an invaluable guide. Bravo!

—*Albert Ellis, Ph.D.*
President
Albert Ellis Institute–New York City

Psychotherapy is an emblematic product of modernity, often accused of participating in the destruction of cultural stability and traditional moral systems of governance. Meanwhile, the core assumptions of psychotherapy alter and change as social institutions perceived as similar lure psychotherapists to reshape psychotherapy to draw on or contrast to the core assumptions of these similar movements. A host of questions is raised: What can we expect from psychotherapy? What can we expect to become of psychotherapy? Woolfolk is an excellent guide through the maze, ranging apparently effortlessly across hermeneutics, interpretative traditions, therapeutic outcome studies, and cultural studies to provide us the perspectives from which answers to these questions can begin to be discerned. *The Cure of Souls* is a systematic, intelligent, perceptive book that will inform those concerned with understanding our culture and challenge those who provide psychotherapeutic interventions to better ground their interventions in what wisdom we can assemble on these issues.

—*John Darley, Ph.D.*
Warren Professor of Psychology
Princeton University

The Cure of Souls

Robert L. Woolfolk

The Cure of Souls

Science, Values, and Psychotherapy

Jossey-Bass Publishers • San Francisco

Substantial discounts on bulk quantities of Jossey-Bass books
are available to corporations, professional associations, and
other organizations. For details and discount information,
contact the special sales department at Jossey-Bass Inc.,
Publishers (415) 433–1740; Fax (800) 605–2665.

For sales outside the United States, please contact your local Simon &
Schuster International Office.

Jossey-Bass Web address: http://www.josseybass.com

Manufactured in the United States of America using Lyons Falls
D'Anthology paper, which is a special blend of non-tree fibers and
totally chlorine-free wood pulp.

The quote on page xiii from *On the Road* by Jack Kerouac is copyright
© 1955, 1957 by Jack Kerouac; renewed © 1983 by Stella Kerouac; renewed © 1985 by Stella Kerouac and Jan Kerouac. Used by permission
of Viking Penguin, a division of Penguin Books USA Inc.

Library of Congress Cataloging-in-Publication Data

Woolfolk, Robert L.
    The cure of souls : science, values, and psychotherapy / Robert L.
Woolfolk.
        p.   cm.—(The Jossey-Bass psychology series)
    Includes bibliographical references and index.
    ISBN 0-7879-4034-8 (alk. paper)
    1. Psychotherapy—Philosophy.   2. Psychotherapy—Social aspects.
I. Title.   II. Series.
RC437.5.W66   1998
616.89´14´01—dc21   97-35057

HB Printing   10 9 8 7 6 5 4 3 2 1   FIRST EDITION

To Lesley

One should not require precision in all pursuits
alike, but in each field precision varies with the
matter under discussion and should be required
only to the extent to which it is appropriate to the
investigation.

—Aristotle

. . . And nobody, nobody knows what's going to
happen to anybody. . . .

—Jack Kerouac

Contents

Preface

Recent developments in the health care marketplace have renewed perennial debates about what forms of psychotherapy are legitimate and effective. Efforts to reduce escalating costs have included an emphasis on brief treatments that (1) are targeted to specific symptom patterns, (2) have been shown effective in empirical studies, and (3) are specific and explicit enough to be described within a treatment manual. Yet many believe that a wholesale movement toward the kind of psychotechnology represented by short-term, manualized treatment is premature and short-sighted, and that it sacrifices the hard-won knowledge gained from a century of the professional practice of psychotherapy.

Within this turbulent context I offer my own investigation into the intellectual and sociocultural underpinnings of psychotherapy—one aimed at shedding light on contemporary controversies. I examine psychotherapy and the disciplines related to it from a number of perspectives: philosophical, sociological, and historical.

Although I am employed as a behavioral scientist and believe the sciences to be exemplary forms of inquiry, I am disturbed by efforts to "medicalize" psychotherapy, to reduce it to a healing technology modeled on somatic medicine. By examining the sociocultural functions of psychotherapy, its value-laden character, its place in the Western tradition of self-examination, and its relation to practical, everyday existence, I argue that there is an inevitable humanistic dimension in psychotherapy, one that resists all efforts to eliminate it. I certainly believe there is a crucial and comprehensive role for scientific modes of thought in the mental health professions, but I also view science as but one dimension of the constellation of social practices that psychotherapy comprises.

Acknowledgments

Had I been able to write this book faster there might be fewer people to thank. But, alas, the list is long. Both Rutgers and Princeton Universities have provided the resources and time to do this work. My long-time chair at Rutgers, Charlie Flaherty, and my psychology department comrades Seymour Rosenberg, John Falk, Stan Messer, and Sandra Harris have been splendid scholarly role models and gracious colleagues. Were it not for the tutelage and other tangible assistance of Arnie Lazarus and Terry Wilson I would never have survived the early years in academia. Terry's encyclopedic knowledge is a scholarly crutch I have leaned on frequently. Over the years I have been fortunate to have as conversation partners such brilliant folk as Frank Richardson, Louis Sass, John Darley, and Mike Gara. Jim Williams, Mabel Allen, and Sherri Irvin deserve special thanks for reading the manuscript and making many helpful suggestions. Leslie Berriman of Jossey-Bass Publishers is a treasure among editors. And were it not for the relentless encouragement, stalwart buttressing, and beguiling companionship of Lesley Allen I could not have completed this book.

Princeton, New Jersey   ROBERT L. WOOLFOLK
December 1997

The Cure of Souls

Chapter One

Introduction

In the United States and increasingly within the economically developed West, psychotherapy is an endeavor that is constantly encountered. The ubiquity of therapy becomes undeniable if one defines it with appropriate breadth to include not only interactions involving mental health professionals but also such technologies of the self as Alcoholics Anonymous, human relations and management training, support groups of various kinds, the diet industry, and Transcendental Meditation, just to name a few. Nor should we fail to mention those omnipresent therapists who disseminate their programs for self-improvement through the various media. Mental health expertise can be found on the Internet, and "virtual" psychotherapy is available there as well (Cutter, 1996). And, of course, there is also the lay therapy practiced by almost everyone on at least someone. So endemic to contemporary life is the therapeutic perspective that its categories and assumptions shape our conceptions of what it is to be human. What were once the controversial assertions of arcane psychological theories now are taken for granted and have become our common sense and conventional wisdom (Nagel, 1994; Wollheim, 1993).

Social Functions of Psychotherapy

Theological, moral, and political explanatory schemes once were the bases of our self-definitions. As these schemes have declined in influence, the interpretation of human nature has come to rely more and more on the kind of explanation provided by behavioral scientists and psychotherapists. The academic discipline of psychology has had considerable impact, supplying a lexicon of psychological concepts to popular culture and a psychological frame of reference to millions of undergraduates every year. Psychotherapy influences directly, through its numerous encounters with clients, and indirectly, through its impact on art, literature, the media, and the multiplicity of social institutions to which psychology and psychiatry are integral.

The widespread effects of psychotherapy would be difficult to comprehend if the various approaches, the "schools of psychotherapy," comprised nothing more than models of psychological functioning and technologies of behavior change. Psychotherapy clearly does more than explain the functioning of the mind. It is more than a set of tools for modifying emotions and patterns of conduct. Psychotherapy also provides a comprehensive guide for living. It tells us what we are, what we can be, and to what we should aspire. Each of the several hundred forms of psychotherapy, in addition to subscribing to a scientific or quasi-scientific psychological theory, also has at its foundation an extensive picture of human existence that is both descriptive and evaluative. Each contains a philosophical anthropology, a comprehensive, multifaceted analysis of human nature that encompasses both scientific and philosophical perspectives. The extrascientific, philosophical dimensions of psychotherapy sometimes are explicit but often are tacit and must be inferred from therapeutic theories, concepts, and practices.

Psychotherapy thus possesses a cultural significance that extends beyond its direct effects on patients and clients. The institution of psychotherapy is a significant source of contemporary customs, values, and worldviews. It is also a sensitive barometer of those same customs, values, and worldviews. The relation between psychotherapy and culture is one of reciprocal influence. Psychotherapy continually absorbs and reflects the culture of which it is a part, while at the same time placing its own distinctive imprint on that culture.

Philip Rieff (1966) labels "therapeutic" those social institutions that correct and redeem and that provide psychological compensations for the pain of life. Rieff maintains that in static, premodern societies the social impact of therapeutic activity is conservative, serving to maintain group solidarity, reaffirm social norms, and reabsorb and reintegrate aberrant individuals into community. In recent times, however, we have borne witness to another capacity of psychotherapy: it also possesses the power to overturn a preexisting set of cultural assumptions when these are at variance with a therapeutic *Weltanschauung*.[1]

All societies past and present have assigned to a designated group of individuals the function of comprehending and contending with deviancy and suffering. The contemporary psychotherapist plays a variant of this role that for millennia has been enacted in many different guises and locales. The strong parallels between psychotherapy and such correlative activities as primitive healing and shamanism have been drawn convincingly and often (Kiev, 1964; Levi-Strauss, 1963). John McNeill (1951) sees analogs of present-day therapy in the moral and spiritual guidance provided to countless people over the centuries by philosophers, sages, clerics, and priests. Indeed, many techniques of contemporary psychotherapy—supportive relationship, dialogue, suggestion, confession, persuasion, reframing, rational problem solving, exhortation, emotional expression, and interpretation of symptoms—also were observed in the various precursors of modern therapy (Frank, 1961; Frank & Frank, 1991).

Although we most commonly think of psychotherapists as healers or counselors, they also function as agents of social control. The clinician is granted responsibility for many bizarre, incapable, or destructive individuals whom the rest of society will not or cannot tolerate. In this context we think most readily of hospitalized, psychotic patients—people afflicted with what was once called madness. In the relation of the mental health professional to madness is found another crucial role of the clinician: guardian of the boundaries of ordinary reality, sentinel on the frontier of psychological fragmentation and oblivion. The therapist is a patroller of the existential night, whose mission is to make psychic demons comprehensible, more familiar, and less terrible.

The social control functions of the mental health professions recently have expanded in the course of their evolving partnership with the judicial and educational systems. Clinicians have become involved in deciding and managing the fates of an increasingly wider range of misfits and malefactors.

Science and Humanism

Throughout the history of psychotherapy much debate has centered on the question of just what kind of enterprise it actually is. The controversy often occurs within the framework of psychology's version of the science versus humanities debate (see Snow, 1970). Is psychotherapy a collection of technologies or, rather, of art forms? Is its ultimate foundation located within the sciences or in the humanities? I shall attempt to provide some partial answers to these questions. The model of psychotherapy I advocate implies that both sides of the humanism-scientism contention are right and that both are also wrong. Each has identified some of what is fallacious in the other position.

The humanists are correct in emphasizing the uniqueness of individual human beings and the difficulty of discovering scientific generalizations that usefully inform our understanding of individual persons. They have produced cogent lamentations on the sterility and simplism of many research findings generated by a behavioral science that imitates a positivistically conceived physical science. The humanists are correct also in their sometimes undeveloped intuitions that psychotherapy can never be reduced to a formulaic technology. Yet for all its virtue as critique, much of the humanistic literature has been characterized variously by anti-intellectual excesses, naïveté about the nature of empirical behavioral science, an exorbitant optimism over human possibilities, and minimal critical self-scrutiny. Scientific investigation is indispensable to a comprehensive understanding of human beings. Even such hermeneutic heroes as Dilthey and Gadamer recognized this. Psychotherapy must have a knowledge base that reflects those warrantable assertions regarding human functioning that have been accumulated by scientifically directed inquiry.

In the pages that follow, I will develop the position that the model of psychotherapy as applied science or psychotechnology, while appropriate to *some* therapeutic activities and objectives, is inadequate to capture the distinctive character of much of what is inevitably involved in psychotherapy. None of the existing humanistic formulations, however, provides a completely satisfactory alternative. I shall argue that philosophical views, most often associated with either hermeneutics or pragmatism, provide supplementary understandings of the human situation that can inform the creation of a more perspicuous and sophisticated model of psychotherapy—one that views it as something more complex than the straightforward application of scientific knowledge to behavior change.

Views that criticize the scientific approach often conceive of psychotherapy as either an art form or, alternatively, a humanistically grounded set of interpretive practices. Neither of these perspectives, however, has unpacked and articulated the inevitable unscientific residual of psychotherapy. I shall argue that therapy is, beyond both the art and science it comprises, an activity involving the development, elucidation, and application of practical knowledge and acumen through dialogue—a form of pedagogy encompassing fact and value, analogous to what in other times has been called the cultivation of character or the development of practical wisdom.

Common Threads

Psychotherapy would appear to be so highly variegated an endeavor that few generalizations apply to it. One is hard pressed to find the common threads that tie together classical psychoanalysis, systematic desensitization, primal therapy, and rational-emotive therapy. But such threads exist. Among these are the social functions common to the different forms of therapy. The manifold therapies all are places to turn in the face of distress, all are regulators of social behavior, and all are constructors of worldviews.

If psychotherapy participates in the construction of cultural Weltanschauung, it most immediately and directly is involved in the construction of many individual realities. In the course of treatment, the therapist must organize and make understandable the concerns of clients by placing those concerns within some coherent explanatory framework. This process of framing and explanation, found in all psychotherapy and therapy analogs from primitive shamanism to the *cura animarum*[2] of the medieval Latin church to contemporary psychoanalysis, necessarily entails a hermeneutic of selfhood. Whether it be a behavior therapist offering a Pavlovian explanation of a snake phobia or an existential therapist interpreting anxiety, in the process of the therapist's explaining the problem, inevitably the self also is explained. Whether I am a deterministically conditioned stimulus-response mechanism with an unfavorable conditioning history or an embodied freedom, a being-for-itself experiencing *angst* in the encounter with finitude, I am, in either case, something explained and understood. An element of self-interpretation is inevitable in all psychotherapy.

Overview of the Contents

The pages that follow contain an extended meditation on the subject of psychotherapy, one that will seek to explore psychotherapy's sociocultural and philosophical underpinnings, to uncover something of its "deep structure." The approach to be employed is interdisciplinary, but most especially extradisciplinary. I want to examine psychotherapy from perspectives outside the mental health professions in order to reveal dimensions of psychotherapy that may not be apparent from within. The aim of this work is an enhanced understanding of the functions of psychotherapy, in the lives of individuals and in the societies they inhabit.

A principal concern of the inquiry will be to scrutinize the intellectual models that have been proposed as most appropriate for psychotherapy. Chapter Two offers a sociocultural analysis of psychotherapy, conceiving of it as an integral aspect of modernity, one engaged in a reciprocal cause-and-effect relationship with contemporary culture. Chapters Three and Four investigate perspectives through which essential features of psychotherapy have been identified. In Chapter Three, I explore the value-laden character of diagnosis and treatment and examine the implications for psychotherapy's claim to scientific status. In Chapter Four, I review two humanistic conceptions of the therapeutic enterprise, those derived from humanistic psychology and from hermeneutics. These are examined in relation to a history of the pursuit of self-knowledge. I explore in Chapter Five the nature of self-understanding in general, and therapeutic self-understanding in particular. Chapter Six is a review of philosophical views that credit and warrant practical knowledge, the know-how of ordinary, everyday existence. Here psychotherapy will be characterized as an integral feature of what phenomenologists call the lifeworld, the arena of practical, mundane activities. Perspectives from pragmatism, analytic philosophy, and hermeneutics are brought to bear on psychotherapy. In Chapter Seven, I shall derive some implications from the earlier analysis for the theory and practice of psychotherapy, assessing the cultural and intellectual status of psychotherapy and offering some speculations on its future.

Chapter Two

Psychotherapy as a Social Institution of the Modern Era

Although primordial forms existed in the earliest human societies, contemporary psychotherapy is a creature of the modern era. It arose, evolved, and achieved its current status in dynamic interplay with forces that created the present world. The growth of psychotherapy from an arcane curiosity into a ubiquitous and influential social institution is part of the story of modernity. Psychotherapy has figured prominently in the modernization of culture, as both a response to and creator of the manifold shifts in custom and belief that our times have witnessed.

Modernization is a term sociologists use to describe the social metamorphoses caused by industrialization and technological innovation, what Karl Polanyi (1957) called the "great transformation" and Alvin Toffler (1980) dubbed the "second wave" in the history of civilization. Modernity refers to the political, economic, and cultural conditions of such transformed societies and is used to contrast the recent West with traditional or premodern society. According to Anthony Giddens (1991), we currently are in the era of late modernity. Some writers (Bell, 1973; Lyotard, 1984) argue that society and culture have entered a postindustrial or postmodern period.[3]

The emergence of psychotherapy can be traced in relation to several processes fundamental to modernization: social fragmentation, individuation, secularization, rationalization, and the rapid expansion and dissemination of knowledge. These processes have resulted in the decline of many traditional institutions (for example, religion, community, and family), whose diverse functions had included providing people with emotional support, regulating their conduct, and furnishing them with a viable worldview. Modernity also witnessed the emergence of new institutions, professions, services, and belief systems whose effects were compensatory and remedial. Psychotherapy is one among these creations of modernity. It has not only assumed the functions of some departed premodern practices, in meeting perennial personal and social needs, but has also provided succor to those affected by the stresses and discontents of the age.

Thus, from one perspective the institution of psychotherapy is a reaction to, or an effect of, modernization. But the relation between psychotherapy and modernity is complex. Psychotherapy assimilates and reflects but also fashions and disseminates modernity. In reciprocal interaction with other elements of society, therapeutic practices and ideologies undergo rapid evolution and then feed back into the main culture, often with profound effects.

The analysis of modernity has preoccupied some of the ablest intellects of the twentieth century and filled thousands of volumes. My treatment of their work will of necessity be highly selective and focused on what is relevant to an analysis of psychotherapy. I intend to focus on three broad classes of development: scientism and secularization, moral subjectivism and relativism, and the rise of the individuated modern self. These categories overlap somewhat but are useful in depicting the principal cultural currents of modernity and their relation to psychotherapy.

A World Disenchanted

Secularization is sometimes thought to be the essential characteristic of modernity (Levy, 1972). To say that modern consciousness is secular is not to suggest that atheism is or will be widespread. It is not and may never be. Secularization refers, rather, to the increasing influence of worldly, as opposed to spiritual, perspectives. Shiner (1967) describes the various components of secularization, each of which is manifested in the contemporary world: the declining prestige and influence of religion, the limitation of religion to the sphere of private life, and an increasing emphasis on temporal activities and perspectives within religious groups.

Max Weber described the premodern world as appearing to its inhabitants as an "enchanted garden." The workings of nature were thought to be imbued with intentionality and spirit. Human beings saw themselves as elements in a purposive, meaningful cosmological order. Human existence was covered by a "sacred canopy" of religious belief, belief that permeated and informed all aspects of everyday life. Speaking in 1918, Weber bore witness to the already evident shift: "The fate of our times is characterized by rationalization and intellectualization and, above all, by the 'disenchantment of the world.' Precisely the ultimate and most sublime values have retreated from public life" (1946, p. 155).

The disenchantment of the world was effected most of all by science, whose stunning successes by the mid-eighteenth century had made it, among the learned, the model for all cognitive activity and the very embodiment of rationality itself. Most Enlightenment thinkers viewed science as an instrument of political liberalism, as a force that would one day permeate all spheres of human activity, advancing liberty and prosperity in the process.

Those humanists of the Enlightenment who saw science as the salvation of humankind no doubt would be astounded and exhilarated by the emancipatory impact of contemporary scientific technology. The power, freedom, and information at the disposal of those in industrialized, high-technology economies are a source of wonder even to ourselves. The great tide of modernity eroded many barriers to individual growth and fulfillment imposed by timeworn ideologies, just as Enlightenment thinkers had hoped and predicted. But in so doing it also washed away much of the cultural glue that had held societies and psyches together.

Almost all premodern people seem to have believed themselves to stand in consequential relation to some transcendental force that controlled the cosmos. The existence of the premodern individual was constituted and made meaningful by virtue of its relation to a cosmological order. The secularization of society has not, however, fundamentally changed human beings so as to eliminate the needs met by premodern cosmologies. Human beings continue to require belief systems that explain social reality and personal existence. They continue to need standards for evaluating and regulating their conduct. Although our contemporary everyday lives radically differ from premodern existence in some ways, there is much in the human situation that is unchanged. Birth, death, marriage, and parenthood remain constants. So do conflicts, quandaries, dissatisfactions, disappointments, and the limited controllability of personal destiny: "Modernity has accomplished many far-reaching transformations, but it has not fundamentally changed the finitude, fragility, and mortality of the human condition. What it has accomplished is to weaken those definitions of reality that previously made the human condition easier to bear" (Berger, Berger, & Kellner, 1973, p. 185).

Premodern belief systems and forms of social organization granted to individuals a sense of belonging, of being at home in the cosmos. To our ancestors, life was comprehensible and had inherent purpose. Modernity changed this sense of life. The decline and disappearance of many traditional institutions created a cultural vacuum. The modern phenomena of social isolation, anomie, and alienation emerged. With characteristic succinctness, Camus (1960, p. 5) described the predicament: "In a universe suddenly divested of illusions and lights, man feels an alien, a stranger. His exile is without remedy since he is deprived of the memory of a lost home or the hope of a promised land."

Into this cultural void has come psychotherapy, a contemporary institution with complex functions. It offers a comprehensive explanation of the human situation, one that has been fashioned in the modern context. The advice and counsel of the mental health professional, as well as the vast psychological literature on the dynamics of human conduct, help us to structure and understand our experiences of suffering and sorrow, to make the pain of life intelligible and thereby easier to bear.

Secular Theodicies

Definitions of reality that make the human condition less onerous, what Weber termed *theodicies*, are hard to come by in a disenchanted world. Though we have not lost our need for belief systems, we have imposed stringent requirements on them. To achieve widespread acceptance, authoritative status, and influence within the public realm, worldviews must be secular. They furthermore must appear to derive from scientific activity and possess scientific or quasi-scientific validity. What have been perhaps the two most influential belief systems of modern times, Marxism and psychoanalysis,[4] initially were avouched by their proponents to be scientific creations. More often than not, detractors have denigrated them by attaching the appellation "pseudoscience."

From the standpoint of the present analysis, Marxism and psychoanalysis each comprises a set of secular theodicies. Their extraordinary durability, despite effective challenges to their scientificity, undoubtedly has to do with their cultural resonances. Each provides both an explanatory scheme and a system of valuation. Each offers a picture of human existence that is compelling and emotionally satisfying. Each also addresses questions of human happiness, self-realization, and redemption.

Marxism is an interesting blend of modern and premodern views. Marx assumes the validity of the Enlightenment values of liberty, freedom, and equality yet describes the realization of such values within a communal system, one of democratic socialism. As did the ancients, Marx locates the fate of the individual in the polis, but then goes on to propose a modern, materialistic explanation of human discontent. Only after the means of production are owned by all, Marx tells us, will human beings achieve their final liberation and full exercise of capacities for self-expression. The solution to the human dilemma is twofold: the restoration of a salutary community (communism) and the reintegration of the individual into that community. In regarding as essential to human prosperity both assimilation of the individual into the community and the subordination of personal needs to corporate purposes, Marxism shares assumptions with both shamanism and religious ideologies.

The analogy between Marxism and religion has been drawn by a number of commentators (Brinton, 1950; Magee, 1982; Nisbet, 1975). Brinton (1950) sees Marxism as an ersatz religion because he is prepared to apply the label *religion* to any "organized and articulate set of beliefs about the Big Questions—right and wrong, human happiness, the order of the universe, and so on—which for the believer did at least two things: gave him intellectual orientation in this world (that is, answered his questions) and gave him emotional participation in a group through ritual and other forms of common action" (pp. 478–479).

Marxism has, in the writings of Marx and Engels, its sacred texts, its orthodoxies and heresies, its god-analog—dialectical materialism—and its kingdom come—the communist commonwealth. The Marxist vision has exercised great power, especially over "several generations of intellectuals bereft of religion and driven thereby into the arms of the waiting church of historical necessity" (Nisbet, 1975, p. 235).

Although psychoanalysis might be classified appropriately as an antireligion, it offers to those who accept its teachings both the theodicies and the directive structures of religion. Psychoanalysis is a philosophical anthropology par excellence—one that is especially eloquent in describing the limitations and possibilities of character and the asperities of the individual's relation to society. The inevitability of human suffering and the indifference and cruelty of fate are well articulated and comprehensively explained. Psychoanalysis creates a picture of life both compelling and inspiring that has endured the rise and fall of competing schools of therapy and remains the most widely accepted therapy among the intellectual elites. Its structure is complex, deep, and grand.

Within the psychoanalytic framework, the ego, the "I," is not the disengaged Cartesian ego of philosophy. The Freudian ego is not as powerful nor as isolated. Freud is neither a self theorist nor an existentialist. For him the quality of life is discovered rather than created, as we come to grips with the limits of our natures and with our powerlessness. Our rational capacities are small and impotent relative to the social and instinctual forces with which we must contend. We need not face the agony of excessive freedom. Our options are limited and therefore our condition secure. We do not confront the cosmos alone. Each human soul is a community of one, composed of distinct and warring parts. In Freud the struggle between good and evil finds its analog in the clash between the primary process of the id and the secondary process of the ego. The struggle of reason to channel the destructive proclivities of the instincts, in Freud's view correlative with the conflict between civilization and barbarism, is enough to fill anyone's heart. For the Freudian, life is not without purpose.

The Secular Ministry

Perhaps psychoanalysis is most accurately described as a transitional explanatory creed, bridging traditional and modern belief systems. Lending support to this view, some observers have suggested that though couched in scientific rhetoric, psychoanalysis retains the mythic qualities of prescientific worldviews. Eliade (1967) has pointed out that the psychoanalytic practice of reviving and "working through" previously unconscious mental contents is in some respects "homologous with the experience of the sacred" (p. 17). For example, the retrieval of memories of early childhood is analogous to the return to the primordial time of myth, the time of the gods that was supposed to have preceded the fall into history. Campbell (1968) sees in psychoanalytic treatment an instantiation of the universal hero-myth. Psychoanalytic treatment becomes a quest in which "[d]epth beyond depth of self-ignorance is fathomed with the analyst in the role of the helper, the initiatory priest" (p. 121).

A thoroughgoing materialist, Freud (1928/1961b) firmly believed that modern human beings must learn to live without the solaces of earlier eras. He was antagonistic to religion and often sought to contrast psychoanalysis with faith. Yet in his later life Freud came to accept certain parallels between the functions of psychoanalysts and those of the clergy. Both provided understanding and consolation to troubled individuals: "Our friends among the protestant clergy, and more recently among the catholic clergy as well, are often able to relieve their parishioners of the inhibitions of their daily life by confirming their faith—after having first offered them a little analytic information about the nature of their conflict. . . . [T]hese procedures . . . have their place in psychotherapy" (1926/1961c, p. 256).

Freud came to believe that a medical education was actually a hindrance to developing psychoanalytic skill. The role of the physician, he thought, was an inappropriate prototype for the practicing psychoanalyst. He offered the term *Seelsorger* (literally "one who cares for souls" but sometimes translated as "pastor" or "minister") as an appropriate appellation describing the function that the analyst performs in relation to the public. The liberation of psychic energy from the snare of repression and the placement of that energy at the disposal of the ego were for Freud "pastoral work in the best sense of the words" (1926/1961c, p. 256).

Freud's rival and intellectual antipode, Carl Jung, embraced with great enthusiasm the parallels between psychotherapy and spiritual direction. In fashioning a humanistic counterpoint to the biological reductionism of Freudian psychoanalysis, Jung came to believe that neurosis was intertwined with the spiritual malaise of a postreligious culture. In Jung's account, modern consciousness is a dispirited, disordered state. The modern individual is cut off from tradition, community, a coherent cosmology. His portrait of the psychotherapy patient is of one "having no love, but only sexuality; no faith, because he is afraid to grope in the dark; no hope, because he is disillusioned by the world and by life; and no understanding, because he has failed to read the meaning of his own existence" (Jung, 1933, pp. 225–226). Jung suggested that modernity produces a psychopathogenic cultural environment, one that forces the psychotherapist into the role of the priest-analogue and requires her to assimilate issues that once were the province of the theologian or philosopher.

Jung's concept of the psychotherapist as secular cleric was taken up by numerous others. Dicks (1950) compared contemporary worldly ideals of mental health with traditional religious goals of "salvation" and "finding God" and likened practitioners of the new behavioral sciences to a temporal priesthood or *therapeutae*. Similarly, Lee (1954) suggested that the modern psychotherapist performs many functions that were previously within the province of the "parish clergyman." Many writers have argued there is a lack of clear distinction between the roles of therapists and clergy, as both provide counsel in the choosing of life goals and in the resolving of morally laden problems of living (London, 1964; Lowe, 1959; Murphy, 1955). There also has been wide recognition that religion and traditional systems of morality, on the one hand, and psychology and psychotherapy, on the other, offer alternative and often competing accounts of the same social and psychological phenomena (Bergin, 1991; Vitz, 1977; Wallach & Wallach, 1983).

Ethics Naturalized

Virtually all of those who made original and significant contributions to psychotherapy—for example, Freud, Ellis, Rogers, Horney, Beck, Wolpe, and Perls—considered themselves to be discoverers of objective, empirical knowledge and viewed psychotherapy as an evaluatively neutral application of that objective knowledge to healing, growth, or behavior change. They did not see themselves as moralists establishing codes of conduct to compete with traditional value systems. Early discord between psychotherapy and conventional values and practices was regarded as conflict between a modern scientific understanding of psychological health and reactionary forces of superstition and ignorance. In *Civilization and Its Discontents* Freud (1930/1961a) described the conflict between the dictates of psychotherapy and those of conventional morality: "We are very often obliged, for therapeutic purposes, to oppose the super-ego, and we endeavor to lower its demands. Exactly the same objections can be made against the ethical demands of the cultural super-ego" (p. 108).

Among the innovators, only Ellis, Jung, and the existentialists anticipated the conclusion forced upon us by the frequent reappearance in the contemporary literature (Cushman, 1995; Fancher, 1995; Lakin, 1988) of the arguments from numerous midcentury critiques (London, 1964; Lowe, 1959; Rieff, 1959): far from being a value-free endeavor, psychotherapy is a morally laden enterprise whose theories presuppose viewpoints both on ideal human functioning and on human baseness and peccability. As Margolis (1966, p. 25) puts it: "[Psychotherapy] is concerned with influencing changes in human action and motivation, a matter that ordinarily falls within the domain of morality. . . . The enterprise of psychotherapy, whatever the variety in doctrinal conviction, clearly presupposes a set of values in the name of which the alteration of the lives of patients is undertaken."

It is not difficult to recognize the moral dimensions of an avowedly philosophical approach to psychotherapy, such as existential therapy, which views itself, in part, as an antiscientific antidote to the discontents of modernity and explicitly endorses a stance of courage and commitment in the face of the uncertain purpose and meaning of our being-in-the-world. The evaluative components of therapies that strive for scientificity and value neutrality are more difficult to pinpoint. But every form of therapy comprises prescriptive as well as descriptive elements. Every system of therapy has an underlying ideology. A therapy may disclose its aesthetic, cognitive, and moral values through the explicit location of thought and conduct on the continuum of health and sickness. Or values may operate tacitly in influencing patterns of therapeutic exploration, in establishing the grounds for therapeutic intervention, or in promoting implicit guidelines for the attitudes and conduct of clients. Each system of therapy has its apotheoses. Psychoanalysis offers the ideal of the genital character, humanistic psychology the self-actualized individual, and cognitive-behavior therapy the rational, assertive individual.

One of the functions of society, according to the sociology of knowledge (Berger & Luckmann, 1966; Mannheim, 1929/1960), is to supply a Weltanschauung, to construct a reality, and in so doing to impose upon experience a framework of meaning. Among the most consequential constituents of societal worldviews are what Nelson (1981) termed *directive structures*, cognitive frameworks that channel and motivate behavior through the articulation of values and norms. Parsons's analogous concept of the *normative order* (1977) refers to the norms and values that maintain social solidarity and regulate social action. The normative order is instantiated in and disseminated by social institutions.

In premodern cosmologies, values are part of the objective order of things, on an epistemological par with facts about nature. One facet of modernity is the erosion of ethical absolutes—a process that subjectivizes and relativizes morality. The traditional morality, for which the therapeutic ethos has surrogated, had been under siege for some time. Morality has had uncertain philosophical grounding among the intellectual elites since the time of David Hume (1739/1950), whose radically empirical philosophy legitimized only the truths of logic and science, and designated all else as "sophistry and illusion."[5] The proliferation of the sensibilities and conclusions of skeptical philosophy among the educated public has left intact few sources of epistemic authority other than science. Thus in a world where little save science has credibility, one crumbling moral order is replaced not by another moral order but rather by a directive system of a different form—a science of conduct, psychology.

Even in societies where values are viewed as ultimately subjective and relative, there is a need for mechanisms that establish what behavior is to be promoted and what is to be proscribed. The institution of psychotherapy and its underlying disciplines are responsive to these societal needs by providing "scientifically grounded" epistemic frameworks for ordering, rationalizing, and norming the social world. The normative order of psychotherapy is one in which fact and value are integrated, often to the extent of being conflated. Psychotherapy effects a transvaluation of values through the naturalization of morality. Sin becomes sickness; virtue becomes health. This translation exemplifies the transformation of consciousness and social roles wrought by modernity: philosopher is supplanted by personality theorist; priest by therapist; magistrate by psychiatrist.[6]

Moral values inevitably entail some assumptions about human capacity. These assumptions involve a conceptual or logical relation in that what we *ought* to do is delimited by what we are *able* to do. Any "ought" implies a corresponding "can." We can be expected to commit and be held accountable for only those acts we are capable of performing (Williams, 1995).

Traditional value systems tended to be based on folk psychologies that set wide limits on human volition. It was assumed that with enough effort anyone was capable of any virtue. Neither the Sermon on the Mount nor the Eightfold Path included the caveat, "Some people may be unable to reach these standards." The scientific, deterministic frameworks of psychology and psychiatry are, to a great degree, incompatible with folk psychology, its libertarian assumptions and corresponding idiom of choice and deliberation. No better evidence of this is available than recent highly publicized murder trials, in which so often it is the frame of reference of the mental health professions that is pitted, on behalf of the defense, against a prosecution that operates within the assumptive world described by ordinary lay language. Every psychiatric explanation, it would seem, potentially offers exemption from responsibility for one's behavior.

The mental health professions thus come to play a "practical" metaphysical role in the lives of citizens, in the course of which they illuminate for the individual those knotty conundra that philosophers have such difficulty solving. Psychotherapy partitions the lifeworld into free and determined, mental and physical. We can learn when we are "being too hard on ourselves" or "expecting too much from ourselves." We can have explained to us whether a sad mood is a by-product of irrational thoughts, childhood trauma, or an imbalance of brain metabolism. Psychotherapy not only offers perspicuous explanation but also grants absolution buttressed by unambiguous scientific finality: "It was not natural; you were not able; it could not have been another way."

The Solitude of One's Own Heart

Critics of the values implicit in psychotherapy are legion. For the most part their critiques have a common understanding of and set of objections to therapeutic ideology, which they deprecate as hedonistic, naturalistic, egoistic, and morally relativistic. Psychotherapy is viewed as exacerbating various problematic aspects of modernity, among them social fragmentation, alienation, and nihilism.

Given the close relationship between modern cultural values and psychotherapy, it is not surprising that many of the arguments directed against psychotherapy are reminiscent of earlier appraisals of modernity by Spengler, Weber, Gehlen, and others. This parallel between the critiques of modernity and those of psychotherapy is unsurprising, given my earlier analysis that argues for viewing psychotherapy as an embodiment of the secularity, humanism, and liberalism of modernity. Several of these critiques of psychotherapy are eloquent laments for a world that is forever lost to us. Some are worth examining in detail.

Rieff and the Therapeutic

Philip Rieff's definitive study (1959) of Freud's thought reveals the founder of psychoanalysis to be a thinker grappling with the problem of modernity. Freud believed that the dawning scientific culture might eventuate in an intrapsychic emancipation of the ego, parallel to the political, economic, and social liberation of the individual achieved during the first phases of the modern era. Yet in

Freud's mind there was the concern that reason alone might be insufficiently powerful to maintain what Freud believed to be the necessary underpinning of all societies—the renunciation of individual instinctual gratification in favor of those superordinate purposes and entities associated with public forms of life. By Freud's time, the elaborate system of repressions that had underlain Western civilization, in the form of Judeo-Christian ethics, had begun to lose its authority and credibility. But for Freud there was no turning back the progression of history. Just as the childhood of an individual must end, Freud believed the cultural childhood of the West was ending. Along with Weber, he saw no option but to face the truth and "bear the fate of the times" with dignity and integrity.

Rieff suggests that Freud's prophesies were prescient, albeit to some degree self-fulfilling. Supervenient to the culture of the past, he contends, is a therapeutic culture, created largely by psychoanalysis and the therapies that came after. In a culture of therapy, the self has been unfettered from its arbitrary and unalterable allegiances to institutions. Freed from "the historic compulsion of seeking large and general meanings for small and highly particular lives" (1959, p. 59), the individual can pursue with sober efficiency the most venerable hedonic imperatives: maximizing pleasure and minimizing pain, and thereby living "with no higher purpose than that of a durable sense of well-being" (p. 40).

Rieff delineates a personification of the current age, whom he calls variously *Psychological Man* or the *therapeutic*. For Rieff, the therapeutic exemplifies the pragmatism and expediency of science, being one who "takes on the attitude of the scientist, with himself alone as the ultimate object of his science" (1966, p. 50). The therapeutic achieves an unprecedented flexibility and plasticity as one for whom "all options ought to be kept alive because, theoretically, all are equally advisable—or inadvisable, in given personal circumstances" (p. 50). No longer bound by absolute moral strictures, the individual is presented with a dazzling array of options.

Although the promise of the new age is great, there are for Rieff attendant perils: serpents in the new therapeutic Eden. The rise of therapy is concomitant with the "impoverishment" of Western culture and its institutions. Infinite possibilities can be difficult to bear. The constant self-focus of an anomic life that is guided by one's own individualistic calculus of pleasure and pain can fragment and destabilize the self.

Here Rieff's analysis is reminiscent of Arnold Gehlen's theory of institutions (1980). In Gehlen's scheme, human institutions are social entities that substitute and compensate for the paucity of instincts possessed by *homo sapiens*, relative to other species. Institutions allow much of life to assume an automatic, "taken for granted" status as habits, rituals, and customs regulate conduct outside of conscious awareness (compare Bourdieu's concept of "habitus," 1990). The failure or decline of institutions means that aspects of social reality believed to be part of the objective order (for example, sex roles) are subjectivized and become objects of conscious reflection. In Gehlen's view, modern institutions that are not legitimized by transcendental authority (psychotherapy, for example) introduce some stability but also, at the same time, tend to destabilize collective traditional institutions, such as the church, by promoting the view that the only rational motive for action is self-interest.

Lasch and Narcissism

Christopher Lasch (1977, 1978) extends Rieff's work to fashion a detailed description of the emotional and psychological consequences of the emergent therapeutic society. His subject is the America of the seventies and eighties, christened by him the Culture of Narcissism. The self-interest of Rieff's therapeutic personality has hypertrophied and become narcissism. Hopelessly egoistic, the narcissist is besotted with self-examination and self-fulfillment. Self-absorbed and hotly pursuing authenticity and awareness, Lasch's member of the Me Generation betrays both an emptiness and a frenetic desperation in which "life becomes a never-ending search for health and well-being through exercise, dieting, drugs, spiritual regimens of various kinds, psychic self-help, and psychiatry. For those who have withdrawn interest from the outside world except insofar as it remains a source of gratification and frustration, the state of their own health becomes an all absorbing concern" (1977, p. 140).

Lasch targets psychotherapy and what he terms the "therapeutic sensibility" for much opprobrium. In his view, therapy has established itself as an antireligion that promotes the destruction of traditional values and the isolation of the individual from meaningful and binding commitments to other persons and institutions. In this universe of therapeutic values, the only legitimate duty is that owed to oneself. Honor involves being true to oneself, presumably after an extensive period of self-discovery. To the therapeutic sensibility, older forms of life, such as self-sacrifice or submission to any authority outside the self, emerge as pathologies. In the Culture of Narcissism mental health entails "the overthrow of inhibitions and the immediate gratification of every impulse" (1978, p. 13).

The Communitarian Critique

A related critique of psychotherapy, again taking its cue from Rieff's seminal work, tends to emphasize the instrumentality and amorality of the therapeutic worldview. Writers such as Alasdair MacIntyre (1981) and the authors of *Habits of the Heart* (Bellah, Madsen, Sullivan, Swidler, & Tipton, 1985) view therapy as infusing attitudes toward oneself and others with a kind of manipulative rationality that focuses entirely on "means" and their effectiveness. This kind of technical reason applied to persons assumes that the "ends" to which therapeutic techniques are applied are preestablished, valid, and outside the scope of therapeutic activity.

For MacIntyre the mode of therapy is prototypical of the amoral stance of modernity. The authority of the therapist derives from the same source as that of another prototypical character of modernity, the manager. That source is the power to achieve results. Managers view themselves as "morally neutral characters whose skills enable them to devise the most efficient means of achieving whatever end is proposed" (MacIntyre, 1981, p. 71). Therapists embody the managerial attitude exported from the public realm to the sphere of private life; they apply it in the service of such taken-for-granted goals as happiness or psychological well-being.

Bellah et al. (1985) link the therapeutic sensibility with an extreme variant of the ethos of American individualism, one that brooks no barriers to psychological autonomy. From the perspective of this radical individualism, an ideal person is one unencumbered by external forces, one whose choices are unconstrained. A corollary proposition is that no value has intrinsic priority over any other. All values, therefore, ultimately are relative and reflexive. In this scheme, commitments to institutions and to other people matter only derivatively. The importance of those commitments is not inherent and is always subject to a revision or recalculation, relative to perceived self-interest.

Bellah et al. (1985) suggest that in the absence of a system of moral beliefs that links individuals nonnegotiably with society, civic life comes to be impoverished. The traditional public sphere, conceived as individual citizens functioning collectively within a community or polis in the pursuit of the common good, cannot be captured adequately by the discourse of therapy. According to Bellah et al. (p. 127), psychotherapy fails to account for "any collective context in which one might act as a participant to change the institutional structures that frustrate and limit. Therapy's 'democratic side' lacks any public forum. Its freedom is closer to the free choice of a market economy than to the shared argument and action of free citizens in a republic." In a related argument, Richard Sennett (1977) has proposed that the combined effects of secularization and consumer capitalism have resulted in a public space that is "dead" and in an ascendancy of the private sphere, where self-gratification predominates.

If we combine the ideas of Sennett and Bellah et al., an ironic interpenetration and reversal of the public and private spheres emerges. Public life, which has lost its meaning when interpreted in terms of collective constructs such as "the general welfare," becomes increasingly personalized in terms that therapeutic selves can relate to. The content of political positions seems less important than the personalities and credibility of those who hold them, the outcome of conflicts less important than the processes of contention among participants. As the distinction between journalism and tabloid journalism begins to blur, so do the boundaries between public and private. Presidents reveal their underwear preferences, and multitudes become voyeurs to the peccadillos and atrocities uncovered in the wake of fallen celebrity. In the private arena, life assimilates the modes of the public marketplace, that is, negotiation and cost-benefit analysis. There is a certain coarsening of commitment to persons and institutions outside the self, given that none is sustained by more than an instrumentally based calculus of utility: "The problem posed by therapy is not that intimacy is tyrannically taking over too much of public life. It is that too much of the purely contractual structure of the economic and bureaucratic world is becoming an ideological model for personal life" (Bellah et al., 1985, p. 127).

Plus ça Change: Tocqueville

When reading Rieff's, Lasch's, and Bellah et al.'s visions of modern American culture, one inevitably is reminded of the standard to which all such accounts are compared, Alexis de Tocqueville's *Democracy in America* (1848/1966). A reading of this masterpiece grants an instant appreciation of just how early the modern situation began to unfold in a nascent United States. An enthusiastic admirer of the American experiment, Tocqueville, nonetheless, was too intellectually penetrating to miss signs of warning. Ever the acute analyst of sociological ironies, Tocqueville suggested that the very features that are most admirable in the modern democratic state ultimately could lead to distasteful consequences.

Equality of opportunity and political power, as well as the plasticity of social structure, produces a society whose bases are individualism and self-interest. Tocqueville tells us that self-interest, although not a "sublime doctrine" that leads to ethical heights, is a necessary foundation of the democratic state. Yet, lamentably, it also is "agreeable to human weakness, and so easily wins great sway. . . . One must therefore expect that private interest will more than ever become the chief if not only driving force behind all behavior" (1848/1966, p. 527).

Tocqueville is optimistic that education can mitigate the undesirable effects of self-interest. Yet he fears that if citizens possessed of true equality "remain ignorant and coarse," there may be no limit to the "stupid excesses to which their selfishness might lead them" (p. 527), nor into what "shameful troubles they might plunge themselves for fear of sacrificing some of their own well-being" (p. 528).

In perhaps the most famous section of *Democracy in America*, Tocqueville establishes himself as one of the earliest critics of modernity. He avers that in dispelling barriers to individual freedom and fulfillment, democracies may erode the ties among people that more authoritarian societies create and maintain, and in so doing, imperil the existential security provided by community. In such circumstances, Tocqueville tells us, genuine contentment is difficult to come by. The individual's capacity to achieve, though great, is not commensurate with the expansive dreams and aspirations fostered by an ideology of limitless opportunity. The price of individual freedom and social mobility, Tocqueville tells us, is emotional isolation: "Thus, not only does democracy make men forget their ancestors but also clouds their view of their descendants and isolates them from their contemporaries. Each man is forever thrown back on himself alone, and there is danger that he may be shut up in the solitude of his own heart" (1848/1966, p. 508).

Rieff, Lasch, and Bellah et al. have many fellow travelers. The bandwagon is capacious and filled with animadversion toward the self-absorption and egoism of therapeutic culture (Butt, 1992; Doherty, 1995; Lerner, 1991; Vitz, 1985; Wallach & Wallach, 1983). For the most part in this discourse, therapy is a proxy for modernity, and whatever animus is directed at therapy seems also to fall upon the modern world.

Rarely do communitarian critiques acknowledge that the fading institutions of the past were imperfect and often functioned to produce results antithetical to their professed values. These critiques frequently are characterized by what Nisbet (1967) referred to as "nostalgia for *Gemeinschaft*," a yearning for the solaces of earlier, simpler, more coherent eras. Often they are predicated on the premise, assumed to be self-evident, that the civilizations of the contemporary West, with that of the United States at the forefront, have begun to decline. Sometimes there is an overestimation of the cultural power of psychotherapy, which is in fact weak relative to such traditional authority structures as church or community.

Despite the palpable appeal of traditional worldviews and their indubitable cosmologies, it is unclear how one would go about resurrecting a lost normative order or whether any past order or facsimile thereof could in fact be instantiated in the current sociohistorical context. The example of that arch-enemy of modernity, Heidegger, who believed that "only a god can save us" from the discontents of modern life, must make us consider the possibility that fantasies of salvation and a wish for absolute directive structures can give rise to waking nightmares.[7]

Psychology and psychiatry, whatever their past and present shortcomings, have important roles to play in the delineation of our current and future concepts of human flourishing. When functioning properly, psychotherapy is, I believe, one valuable component of our cultural quest to find durable and credible sources of self-understanding in an age during which much that was solid has melted into air. Therapy has, in fact, served to promote a liberal, tolerant normative order, one that endorses the values of the contemporary democratic state: equality of personal rights, freedom of action, unconstrained discourse, and respect for diversity. In addition, all forms of psychotherapy, with the possible exception of those that have recently adopted "social constructionist" meta-theories, elevate to a Socratic level the importance of self-understanding and the pursuit of truth, both about oneself and the world. Freud, Jung, Adler, and the greats who followed believed psychotherapy to be an activity with intrinsic merit: a pathway to knowledge and enlightenment. The values of democracy coupled with the mission of finding truth are, for some, a meager and debased substitute for the certainties and consolations of times past. Yet they are sufficient to confer meaning and purpose on the lives of some seekers and to comfort people who do not demand surety of this existence.

Psychotherapy: A Modern Service Industry

There are numerous perspectives that can be brought to bear upon the role of psychotherapy in modern societies. One such viewpoint is that of economics, from which psychotherapy emerges as a burgeoning profession and service industry.

As mentioned earlier, one feature of modernity is accelerating economic growth and complexity. As societies advance economically, a progressively smaller fraction of commerce is devoted to basic subsistence. People come to desire this year's new model automobile, a personal fitness trainer, or nonspotting dishwashing detergent not out of necessity but rather because of tastes that are fabricated by the culture. Demand for such goods and services can arise through word of mouth or through their depiction or promotion in the various information media.

From the perspective of economics, psychotherapy is a service industry, one that seems to address both perennial needs and some that recently have been socially constructed. It is analogous to the fast-food industry, which satisfies a basic human requirement in a contemporary vein, through techniques adapted to the values and lifestyles of today. Psychotherapy is also similar to various forms of consultation, such as financial planning, in that the activity is predicated on a modern sociohistorical situation without which there would be no need for the service.

Since World War II the structure of the U.S. economy has been shifting. The labor force involved in manufacturing and agriculture has been shrinking while the proportion of the economy devoted to services that are perceived to enhance life has been increasing. In the period from 1959 to 1989, the number of health service workers quadrupled and those delivering business services increased sixfold (Spulber, 1995).

The mental health professions are growing at a rate much faster than that of the general population. At current rates of growth the number of clinical psychologists will double every ten years, social workers every fourteen years, and psychiatrists every twenty years (Dawes, 1994). Between 1957 and 1976 the use of mental health professionals tripled, whereas consultations with clergy or nonpsychiatrist physicians for help with "problems of living" increased at much slower rates (Veroff, Kulka, & Douvan, 1981).

From 1970 to 1989 the percentage of workers with some higher education increased from 26 percent to 46 percent (Spulber, 1995). White-collar workers increased from 37 percent of the labor force in the 1950s to 57 percent by the end of the 1980s. This growing "educated, white-collar" section of the population is the principal market for psychological services. College graduates are twice as likely to consult a psychologist or psychiatrist than individuals with no college education, and are three times as likely to do so as individuals who have not gained a high school diploma (Veroff, Kulka, & Douvan, 1981).

Jerome Frank (1973) has observed that the demand for psychotherapy seems to increase as a function of its availability. Is there a cultural vacuum of such size that no number of mental health professionals would be sufficient to fill it? Clearly the proliferation of therapy has the effect of further "psychologizing" society, thus creating demand for therapy by sensitizing people to their emotional discomforts, establishing a psychological idiom and frame of reference for understanding life, and creating life expectations whose realization requires psychotherapy. Karl Jaspers (1964, p. 8) suggested many years ago that "therapeutic schools unwittingly foster the phenomena which they cure." In a related observation, Jacques Ellul remarked that contemporary technology evolves independently of human needs, often creating "solutions" for which there are not yet problems (1965, p. 89).

The sociohistorical analysis of psychotherapy provided earlier in this chapter has been weighted heavily toward a conception of psychotherapies as systems of cultural meanings and as structures of social direction, constantly interacting with the society at large. This perspective is useful, as far as it goes, yet it provides an incomplete account of how psychotherapy evolves. Psychotherapy not only affects and is affected by the social sphere of which it is a part, but it also is driven by internal dynamisms. Transformations, be they discoveries or changes of fashion, often result from activities internal to a profession or discipline. Psychotherapy comprises technologies and systems of expertise, whose mavens function as professional practitioners and knowledge workers. Their activities are, in many respects, autonomous, serendipitous, generative. The field is part of the larger culture, but also is a subculture with its own innovative momentum.

In the following chapter I explore the claim of psychotherapy to belong to that category of expert knowledge regarded as most legitimate in our culture.

Chapter Three

Psychotherapy and the Integration of Science and Values

Since it separated from philosophy at the end of the nineteenth century to become an independent discipline, psychology self-consciously has sought to fashion itself as science. Despite early doubts concerning the scientific status of psychoanalysis, which have persisted to the present day, Freud continued to insist on the essential scientific character of his creation. The ascendancy of perhaps the foremost competitor of psychoanalysis on the contemporary therapeutic scene, cognitive-behavior therapy, can be credited largely to the therapy's claim to have more truly embodied the standards and methods of science than any of its predecessors. Even various phenomenologists—for example, Rogers (1964) and Giorgi (1970)—have defended their opposition to the mainstream, not by repudiating the ideals of science in favor of those of literature or magic but by asserting that they had discovered the proper methodology for a "new" science of human beings.

A scientific approach to psychotherapy ostensibly would seem to be the most appropriate means of realizing what most who seek therapy expect it to be: an effective remedy for their maladies. Empirically demonstrated efficacy is what most tough-minded intellectuals as well as most consumers expect from any therapeutic endeavor, whether it be brain surgery or chiropractic. It is possible, of course, to have healing techniques that are effective but that nevertheless are rationalized within the rubric of a spurious explanatory system. Much primitive healing and many current healing practices, such as acupuncture and faith healing, frequently are assumed to have some practical efficacy but have an invalid explanation of the mechanisms of that efficacy. One could argue that this is where we stand with most forms of psychotherapy. Each is somewhat effective when applied to the kinds of diffuse problems typical of therapy outpatients. The overall success rates of the various approaches appear to be somewhat comparable (Seligman, 1995; Smith, Glass, & Miller, 1980). But the theories that underlie the various therapies are dissimilar, so divergent that they cannot all be true.[8]

If psychotherapy were a genuine scientific technology, it would be both practically effective and grounded within a valid knowledge base, one that develops quasi-cumulatively and contributes to application, in the manner of the established sciences. A foundation science of this sort makes its own successful claim to truth, independent of the successes of any associated technologies. Here the model technology of healing is somatic medicine, whose practices derive from the basic sciences of biology, which themselves are continually generating new knowledge from which novel medical applications are derived. Although the pretension of psychotherapy to be an effective pragmatic technology is increasingly secure (Bergin & Garfield, 1994), opinion remains divided on the success of its foundational science, psychology, and on the nature of the relationship between the discipline of psychology and the field of psychotherapy.

The wish to achieve scientific status is related to another perennial and ubiquitous aspiration of the mental health professions, that of objectivity and value-neutrality. Those who subscribe to the partitioning of fact and value—a position that comes to us from Hume's positivism and Weber's dream of value-free (*wertfrei*) social science—assert that science and values are incompatible and irreconcilable. On this account, science must be disinterested and impartial. And for an activity to qualify as science, it must be devoid of prescriptive content.

In the previous chapter I argued that the putative value-neutrality of psychotherapy is, in practice, a myth. In this contention I am one among an expanding multitude (Bellah et al., 1985;

Cushman, 1995; Fancher, 1995; Lowe, 1959). I also made a stronger claim, that all therapeutic systems contain disguised ideologies. There is a stronger claim yet, which I endorse: any conceivable form of psychological diagnosis or treatment is inevitably and necessarily value-laden. If true, this last contention might, for many, rule out the possibility that psychotherapy could qualify as an applied science.

My final claim regarding the inevitable value-laden character of theory and practice within the mental health profession, and the implications of this claim for the scientific status of psychotherapy and psychodiagnosis will be the subjects of this chapter. In exploring this material I shall not seek to define science precisely. I am convinced by the recent philosophy of science that it is folly to attempt to identify the essence of science or to predict, for any discipline, what practices and paradigms will lead, ultimately, to the kind of certitude and achievement characteristic of the "successful" sciences, for example, physics (Laudan, 1984).

Rather than engage in a systematic and comprehensive analysis, I offer instead several "case studies" of attempts to cope with the problem of values within the fields of psychology and psychiatry by those who sought to establish and confirm the scientific status of those fields. Although none of the efforts was entirely successful, a close examination of each reveals some facets of the complex relationship between values and psychotherapy and, I believe, provides support for my assertion that, in both treatment and diagnosis, values are unavoidable.

Biological Psychiatry: Materialism Again

Modern biological psychiatry (Guze, 1992; Wender & Klein, 1981) contends with the evaluative dimension of psychiatric categorization by essentially denying it in favor of a naturalistic, materialistic conception of psychopathology. The contemporary medical model seeks to objectivize diagnostic categories by an act of biological reductionism. Researchers and theorists in this field pursue the laudable aims of uncovering relationships between patterns of symptoms, on the one hand, and genetic factors or discernible metabolic processes that can be manipulated pharmacologically, on the other hand. They then go on to identify psychopathology with its associated biology.

The earlier psychoanalytically based medical model, which dominated psychiatry during the fifties and sixties and analogized between dysfunctional psychodynamics and dysfunctional somatic processes, argued that mental illnesses were *like* physical diseases. Mental illnesses manifested emotional and behavioral "symptoms" that were the result of unconscious psychological conflicts. This psychoanalytic medical model was criticized on a number of bases, one of which was the assertion that the analogy of physical and mental illness was false. Some of the most effective criticism involved the claim that applying labels such as *normal, pathological,* or *healthy* to human conduct inevitably entails a value judgment about the way people live and think. This normative aspect of psychiatry worried many observers who feared and abhorred the possibility that psychiatry might become a source of social values or an instrument of political oppression.

The current biopsychiatric medical model attempts to avoid any such troublesome ethical implications by asserting that mental illness literally *is* physical illness. Mental diseases are bona fide diseases. They are exactly the same as physical diseases in all important respects. Entities such as depression are diseases, in the way that tuberculosis and cancer are. All are, in essence, malfunctions of physical processes, malfunctions that eventuate in disease symptomatology. By defining "mental illness" in terms of underlying physical processes, rather than by using behavioral or experiential criteria, it is presumed that psychodiagnosis can be made objective and that judgments of value can be eliminated.

Contemporary biopsychiatrists fall prey to what proves to be a spurious assumption: that by drawing a sharp distinction between mental and physical causes of mental illness and addressing only those causal processes that are physical, the cultural bias in disease nosologies can be eradicated and the objective, scientific status of psychiatric diagnostic labels thereby secured. Curiously, such critics of mainstream psychiatry as Szasz (1983) and Goffman (1961) accept a portion of this assumption and wind up being inadvertent ideological fellow travelers with the biological psychiatrists—but on the other side of the same objectivist coin. The anti-psychiatrists essentially accept the same positivistic viewpoint as do the biological psychiatrists and assume that a partitioning of the biosocial world into psychological and somatic domains allows us to sort human issues into the corresponding spheres of morality and science, value and fact, respectively. Reasoning within both movements assumes that physical disease represents some value-free, naturalistic, unproblematic class, whereas mental dysfunctions are fundamentally value judgments. For example, Szasz asserts that so-called mental illnesses are pseudo-illnesses, conditions that do not belong to the same logical class as physical illnesses, which, he contends, are describable in the value-free idiom of the natural sciences.[9]

What both biological psychiatry and anti-psychiatry fail to grasp is that no straightforward partitioning of human maladies into the categories of the physical and mental is possible, and that even if it were, such a distinction would not correspond to a division between real and pseudo diseases. The reality of the matter is that all of what are termed diseases (in either psychiatry or physical medicine) have a combination of mental and physical characteristics. A strep throat has, along with invading bacteria and reddening of the upper esophagus, the subjective properties of pain and "feeling sick." Similarly all mental illnesses, indeed every mental activity, every thought and feeling, are correlated with an underlying set of physical events. A schizophrenic's hallucinations do not originate in some mental ether, but rather in the biology of the brain. When we examine illnesses from the various standpoints of etiology, symptomatology, and treatment, they emerge as complex entities with multifaceted, interacting components. Contemporary biobehavioral conceptions of illness emphasize the importance of lifestyle, attitudes, social relations, and other such morally laden aspects of living in the etiology

and treatment of many physical diseases. The advent of such disciplines as behavioral medicine and psychoneuroimmunology has
brought us evidence on the close connections and complex interactions among mental, behavioral, and somatic variables in many
domains of medicine.

Even if we could in some way marginalize the psychological and
behavioral aspects of psychopathology, we would not eliminate the
social, historical, and moral dimensions of psychiatric illnesses. The
reason for this inability has to do with the concept of illness itself.
As Sedgwick (1982) has pointed out, it is intellectually justifiable to
place mental and physical diseases in the same category, but not
because we have generated culturally inert, value-free descriptions
of psychopathological processes entirely within the terminology of
physiology or biochemistry, as biological psychiatry would have it.
Ironically, we are able to place mental and physical illness on the
same footing because an examination of the logical structure of
judgments regarding health and sickness reveals the nature of all illness and all treatment as prescriptive social constructions (Veatch,
1973). Sedgwick (1982, pp. 30–31) states: "Out of anthropomor-
phic self-interest, we have chosen to consider as 'illnesses' or 'diseases' those natural circumstances that precipitate the death (or the
failure to function according to certain values) of a limited number
of biological species: ourselves, our pets and other cherished live-
stock, and the plant varieties we cultivate for gain or pleasure."

There are no diseases in nature in the way that there is mass,
velocity, or atomic structure. To characterize a process as a disease
is to weave it into a complex web of social meaning that comprises
both norms of evaluation and technologies of remediation. Natural
events become instances of health or illness only after human
beings intervene with their systems of classification. "The fracture
of a septuagenarian's femur has, within the world of nature, no
more significance than the snapping of an autumn leaf from its
twig: and the invasion of a human organism by cholera germs carries with it no more the stamp of 'illness' than does the souring of
milk by other forms of bacteria" (Sedgwick, 1982, p. 30).

Applying the disease label is simply a value judgment! Disease is a social construction! How can this be? Physical illnesses seem clearly part of nature, and medicine seems methodologically impeccable, a shining example of applied science. We intuitively want to point to the qualitative differences between physical and mental illnesses, in part because the former seem not to be affected by cultural variation in the way that the latter appear to be. For example, malaria is malaria, a disease, in any society; its status as a conceptual and empirical entity seems not in any important sense to be influenced by cultural factors. But narcissistic personality disorder not only seems to emerge as a consequence of social developments (for example, the eroding of sociocentric concepts of identity) but also is a phenomenon whose very placement in the category of the pathological is a result of societal norms. The issue here is not whether mental disorders can be more arbitrarily designated than physical ailments or whether there is generally less cross-cultural consensus on mental disorders. We need no more unsettling example than that of mid-twentieth-century Soviet psychiatry to illustrate the malleability of the categories of psychopathology and their great potential for political exploitation.

That there is almost universal agreement on the pathological status of many conditions that share the label *physical disease* does not demonstrate the objective status of the category. It only shows that people universally fear and have distaste for death and infirmity and those conditions that bring them on. Another example of an analogous universal attitude is the uniformity across diverse societies in the proscription of murder. We find at least as much cross-cultural consensus on the proposition "Murder is a crime" as we do "Cancer is a disease." But no one would contend that laws against murder are not social constructions just because all societies have them. Nor would anyone suggest that there is no value judgment implicit in making certain homicides crimes just because such value judgments are virtually universal. Both crime and disease are evaluative, prescriptive categories that are socially constructed.

Those clinicians who seek to make psychotherapy an applied science, however, are accurate in their assumption that certain biobehavioral regularities are fundamental to human conduct. Even at the primitive state of current knowledge, some generalizations about "pathological" behavior can be made. If I encounter a patient with bipolar affective disorder in the throes of a manic episode and do not assume that some chemotherapeutic intervention would be the most effective means of attenuating the manic symptoms, I fly in the face of an overwhelming preponderance of research data. Similarly, in the case of a circumscribed phobia, if a therapist eschews methods that include imaginal or in vivo exposure to the feared stimulus, he is ignoring a set of facts on a par with water's proclivity to run downhill. The behavior therapists cogently presume that certain aspects of psychotherapy are very much like engineering. When variables are identifiable and manipulable, when the linkages to feelings and behavior are robust (suggesting palpable and straightforward underlying mechanisms), then the therapist can pull the levers, push the buttons, and await a probable but not certain outcome, as does any other technician.

What biological psychiatry has gotten right is that all human activity has a biological substrate. Someday it may be possible to produce a well-founded neurochemical and neurophysiological account of the etiology and dynamics of such syndromes as schizophrenia. We ultimately may even develop fine-grained neurobiological analyses of the processes that underlie and "cause" such discrete human acts as the typing of keystrokes on a computer. How far behavioral neuroscience will progress is an empirical question that only time can answer. But anyone who doubts that an underlying biology, in some critical fashion, gives rise to thoughts, feelings, and behavior is arguing, in effect, for the causal independence of events we currently classify as psychological and somatic (Searle, 1984). Unless we are prepared to assume that ice picks driven into the cortex would produce no mental consequences, such a view is indefensible.

But even if we grant that a complete account of the biological underpinnings of behavior can be given at the level of brain mechanisms, the theoretical reducibility of the psychological to the biological would not amount to a practical reduction. In most cases it would be about as useful to a therapist as knowledge of quantum mechanics is to a civil engineer. Although concrete and steel are made up of atoms that comprise even smaller and more evanescent entities, knowledge of subatomic physics does not help us build bridges. It is, at the practical level of much engineering science, irrelevant. Similarly, in the realm of human psychology, we can assume that all psychological life may be, in principle, reducible to brain biology without our also maintaining that a neurobiological technology of behavior control can be developed. After all, we can explain scientifically many phenomena (such as the weather) that we can neither control nor predict with exactitude.

More certain is that the biological level will not replace the psychological as the medium of self-understanding and discourse. Its theories and constituent concepts simply do not connect with most worlds of human practice at the levels those worlds are conceived and carried out. Just as bridge builders will never talk much to each other about quarks, is it unlikely that declarations in ordinary language, such as "I love you," will ever be replaced by what would doubtlessly be a very elaborate, lengthy, and unromantic description of limbic system excitations.

Let us go a step further, grant the science fiction writer her due, and deem it feasible that brain-state cartographers can give us a set of neural coordinates such that for every statement like "My left elbow itches," there is some digitized translation that represents the corresponding neurobiology, "TY32-x697FL-42r," perhaps. We could, presumably, start communicating with these symbols instead of with English words. Let us also assume that each of is equipped with a brain stimulator that could be dialed to a setting that would produce whatever feelings or behaviors we desired, so long as these were within the organismic capacity.

Even in this hypothetical world possessed of a completely effective psychotechnology, we would not have removed all but "objective" scientific description and explanation from the lifeworld. This is because in our hypothesized future, people still would be required to operate the brain stimulators, to decide when to use them and on what settings they should be placed. Of course, one might assume that we would simply dial up "feel good" and keep the setting right there, but I would argue this to be an unlikely scenario. People in our real world of today often do not choose what they know to be immediately pleasurable. Would pleasure be as desirable, and would it have the same significance for us, if we could command it? How would we feel about ourselves in such a world? Would some unsuspected malaise befall a people so capable of self-manipulation? With so many emotional options and potentially limitless possibilities for discourse and reflection on the value and proper role of pleasure in life, might there not still be work for psychotherapists to do?

The kind of work that might remain for therapists in our futuristic fantasy world would have to do with that aspect of psychotherapy that is *not* technological. The technological dimension of psychotherapy involves bringing about ends that are deemed desirable. The task that would remain in our world of the future is the exploration, examination, and, most important, the *selection* of the ends themselves, a task that never can be achieved by technology alone.

A Critique of "Pure" Technology: The Case of Behavior Therapy

The history of behavior therapy provides us with an instructive example of the difficulties inherent in attempts to erect a value-free technology of behavior change. No other system of psychotherapy sought so self-consciously to establish itself as a "pure" technology. Its ultimate failure to produce a completely objective form of treatment resulted not from the lack of zealous effort but from the inability of any psychotechnology to divest itself entirely of prescriptive elements.

Behavior therapy was viewed by its originators as an evaluatively neutral body of objective knowledge, verified by empirical research. Behavior therapy's self-image was that of an applied science, devoid of any prescriptive thrust or ideology. A leading textbook on behavior therapy provided the following definition: "As an applied science, behavior therapy is simply a collection of principles and techniques about how to change behavior; it says nothing about who should modify what behavior, why, or when" (Wilson & O'Leary, 1980, p. 285). So widely accepted was the characterization of behavior therapy as a pure technology, as means potentially capable of serving any political or cultural end, that much concern was aroused that behavioral technology might function effectively in the service of totalitarian political regimes bent on the restriction of personal freedoms (Woolfolk, Woolfolk, & Wilson, 1977). Depictions of perverse applications of behavioral technology were widespread, notably in the novels *Brave New World* and *A Clockwork Orange*.

Behavior therapy sought to remain neutral with regard to what would constitute an ideal or optimally functioning person. The therapeutic goals of other, earlier varieties of psychotherapy had been provided by theories of personality and psychopathology that defined "healthy" and "unhealthy" psychological functioning. But the kind of comprehensive theory of human needs and propensities that infused earlier systems of psychotherapy with prescriptive thrusts was antithetical to the behavioral approach.

In its first years, behavior therapy favored explanations of behavioral dysfunction derived from conditioning theory that emphasized the external, situational, and observable determinants of behavior. Mischel's critique (1968) of classical personology and psychodiagnosis argued powerfully against the coherence of behavior across situation and circumstance. This work was widely read and so frequently cited by behavior therapists that it came to be regarded as a basic text in the field. Behavior therapy rejected trait-based conceptions of human behavior in favor of a complex "cognitive social learning theory" (Bandura, 1977; Mischel, 1973) that was putatively neutral with respect to what would constitute a personal ideal or an ideal person. Rejection of the medical or disease model of psychopathology, including traditional psychiatric diagnostic categories, was so central to behavior therapy that it was frequently cited as a defining characteristic of the approach (Kazdin, 1978).

Behavior therapists were purists and extremists. Their distrust of and skepticism toward psychiatry and psychoanalysis enabled them to generate cogent criticisms of psychiatric nosologies contained in *DSM-I* and *DSM-II*. Many went further and accepted Szasz's view that mental illness was a myth, or, at the very least, a purely social construction. Sometimes the acceptance of such radical ideas proved to be uncritical and led to intellectual excesses. We find such judicious scholars as Ullmann and Krasner (1969) one-upping the anti-psychiatrists by asserting that all psychodiagnostic categories are social constructions and that psychopathology is nothing more than the enactment of "roles." These roles, they argue, are created by the labels employed by a psychiatric power structure. Psychopathology becomes simply "behavior that is unexpected and upsetting to some person powerful enough" (p. 102) to exert control over that behavior. This co-opted anti-psychiatry perspective was wedded to the view that all human conduct derives from processes of conditioning. We see leading behavior therapists boldly pronouncing schizophrenia to be a social role comprising learned responses, developed through the very same mechanisms that give rise to such more standard acquisitions as table manners or golf swings: "Abnormal behavior is no different from normal behavior in its development, its maintenance, or the manner in which it may eventually be changed. The difference between normal and abnormal behaviors is not intrinsic; it lies rather in the societal reaction to them" (Ullmann & Krasner, 1969, p. 92).

Such views resulted in part from identifying the science of human behavior with research on habit acquisition in laboratory animals and, also, from the importation into the behavior therapy movement of the behaviorist, environmentalist ideology that was the foundation of conditioning theory. Some of what appears to us now as uncritical intellectual extremism had to do with the shared antipathy of anti-psychiatrists and behavior therapists toward the dogmatism and authoritarianism of midcentury psychiatry. Both behavior therapy and anti-psychiatry were polemical reform movements with similar ethical agendas. Both were bent on enhancing the liberty of individuals unlucky enough to find themselves in the thrall of what was deemed a body of superstition and pseudoscience.

After these points of agreement the movements diverged. Szasz consigns what psychiatrists label psychopathology to the realm of morality and social deviance. He explicitly removes psychopathology and psychotherapy from the purview of science. For behavior therapists, however, a science of psychopathology and a technology of therapy, absent the metaphor of disease, can and should be created out of conditioning theory and built on the ruins of psychodynamic psychiatry. By eschewing the medical or disease model of psychological dysfunction, behavior therapy divested itself of the global, evaluative labels that have defined, in other systems of therapy, which persons are in need of treatment and what the aims of treatment are.

No systematic body of knowledge that is applied to concrete human situations can evade the issue of goals. In the case of behavior therapy the question of therapeutic goals took the following form: If we have no theory of psychopathology to establish the desiderata of human existence or to guide our clinical activities, how do we decide when and where to act? The answer given by behavior therapy was the simple, straightforward implication of its underlying ideology: therapeutic goals are a matter for the client to decide.

Behavior therapists were, in fact, radical democrats on the issue of therapeutic goals. The client was envisioned as a consumer. The therapist was assumed to possess no special wisdom regarding life direction. She was regarded as a flexible, amoral behavioral engineer. Therapy was conceptualized as a contractually based and freely chosen application of the technology of behavior change to oneself, albeit mediated through the rather straightforward and transparent ministrations of a technician-therapist: "The behavior therapist has no . . . such normative concepts as health and sickness, growth and stagnation, which in other systems transcend the preferences of the individual. . . . One might, in fact, argue that this is a principal ideological vector of behavior therapy: to dispense with perspectives that limit the rights of individuals to pursue self-chosen goals in the most expedient manner science can produce" (Woolfolk & Richardson, 1984, p. 783). The ideological function of this ostensible neutrality with respect to the content of therapeutic objectives, however, was not to eliminate values from therapy, as intended, but rather to promote those "formal" liberal democratic values so familiar to us all: tolerance, equality, and freedom.

Behavior therapy adopted from its inception what has been variously termed the technological attitude (Berger & Kellner, 1981) or technocratic consciousness (Gouldner, 1976). Its goal was the rational, predictable control of events—the aim of all technology. The ideological bias of technology is in the emphasis of form over content, means over ends, methodology over theory (Winner, 1977). Efficacy, replicability, and specificity are its cornerstones. The criteria of technology on the surface may appear to be ideologically neutral. Yet they are, in fact, cognitive values the allegiance to which can render illegitimate alternative, putatively less "efficient" forms of intellectual and practical activity that may have different aims and methods (Ellul, 1965). One aspect of the technological attitude is the ascendancy of rationality and logic over intuitive and emotional functions: "the exclusion of all that is purely traditional, charismatic, or ritualistic, all, in short, that is not directly related to the means necessary to efficient realization of a given end" (Nisbet, 1976, p. 111).

The sensibility of behavior therapy has always been Apollonian, as opposed to Dionysian. Mahoney (1980) criticized behavior therapists for their overly narrow view of emotionality, stating that for behavior therapy, feelings are phenomena to be "averted, regulated, or otherwise controlled" (p. 167). Behavior therapy placed little emphasis on the cultivation of the passions, spontaneity, and aesthetic sensitivity, goals that are given considerable emphasis in other approaches to psychotherapy. Behavior therapy advocated the life of reason, balance, self-control, and objectivity.

And although it eschewed any explicit description of the healthy or optimal individual, behavior therapy nevertheless necessarily had its implicit conception of the healthy person: one who could effectively employ behavioral technology. This ideal person is one free from the irrational influence of excessive emotion, an assertive (not aggressive) and pragmatic individual who can choose objectives, stick with those choices, and responsibly carry out those activities necessary for their realization.

Having It Both Ways: Science and Values

What follows are two attempts not to eliminate values but to recognize and assimilate values into scientific approaches to treatment and diagnosis.

Objectivizing Value

Another kind of response to the discovery of the prescriptive underpinnings of much activity within the mental health professions is, in some sense, the opposite of the tack taken by biological psychiatry and behavior therapy. Whereas these latter approaches attempt to segregate themselves from values, another alternative is to *embrace* the normative aspects of psychiatry and psychotherapy. This outlook, in its most general form, seeks to identify the values underlying the mental health professions and then to justify those values, often by some appeal to the methods or findings of empirical science.

Bergin's writing on psychotherapy and religious values (1980, 1985, 1991) is an eloquent example of this genre. Bergin is aware of the literature showing that psychotherapy is a social influence process in which even "nondirective" therapists' values can be identified (Murray, 1956; Truax, 1966), and, during the course of which, clients' values shift in the direction of their therapists' (Beutler & Bergan, 1991; Kelly, 1990). Bergin is untroubled by these findings, because he envisions a role for the psychotherapist that openly acknowledges psychotherapy as a pedagogy of valuation: "When we reconstrue the psychotherapist's role as one of evaluating and guiding value decisions . . . we are entering a sensitive domain. But it is a domain through which I believe we are likely to have a more positive and lasting influence. In effect, this means bringing values into our traditional rational and empirical framework" (1985, p. 114).

Bergin argues that facts and values can work synergistically within therapy. He avers very credibly that values are constituents of the individual's worldview that may play a causal role in psychopathology, much as other cognitive and attitudinal factors do. In fact, Bergin suggests that we should use research methods to subject therapeutic values to empirical "test, criticism, and verification," thereby determining the values whose promotion would result in health and happiness. Armed with information about the empirical relationships among values and aspects of mental health, the therapist, putatively, can advance those values that are warranted by science to produce salutary therapeutic outcomes.

For several reasons, however, "verifying" values in the sense that Bergin intends is a highly questionable undertaking. Now it so happens that the values Bergin prefers most, and wishes to argue for most strongly, are those of the Judeo-Christian tradition. As an example, he states that it would bolster the legitimacy of religious values if it could be shown that participation in religious communities results in lower rates of social and emotional pathology and physical disease. According to this argument, if belonging to a congregation results in lower cholesterol, less depression, and so on, then we have produced evidence in support of the religious value system involved. Bergin does then, in fact, present a well-developed argument to the effect that traditional religious values are "good for one's health," in addition to their other virtues.

Bergin's program advises us to determine whether certain ethical positions seem to promote mental health. Assuming that we can agree on the standards of mental health, this question, in principle, may be answerable through empirical studies. But there are logical problems involved in attempting to justify moral values by this particular empirical exercise. The various definitions of mental health are themselves underlain by values. If we use the norms of mental health as criteria for the justification of traditional moral codes, how then are we to justify those values implicit in norms of mental health? If we accept mental health as the standard by which values will be measured, we cannot then "verify" the values implicit in the norms of mental health without arguing in a circle. One way to avoid logical circularity is to accept the mental health values of happiness and well-being as self-evidently valid and ultimate. But this move clearly has the effect of *undermining* the traditional values it is designed to uphold, by relegating them to a secondary, derivative status.

There are further difficulties, of a practical sort, involved in attempting to justify traditional morality on the basis of its instrumental effects. For example, if we decide that our values will be based on whether those values will make us happy, we place ourselves in a kind of practical predicament. Is a moral belief entered into for extrinsic reasons really equivalent to one held for intrinsic reasons? I may choose to go on a low-cholesterol diet because it can be demonstrated that this improves my chances of avoiding coronary heart disease. But if it can be shown that believing in a supreme being similarly reduces cardiovascular pathology, can I elect to believe in God in the same way that I choose to embark on a diet? In the first place, if studies showed a positive correlation between religious belief and health, and even if we could infer from such data that religious belief *causes* enhanced health, these studies would be of limited utility to therapists wishing to present religion to clients as a tool for promoting well-being. Such studies, of course, are not conducted on individuals who have chosen their religious beliefs for instrumental reasons. They are studies of "true" believers, people who hold the views they do because they think the views are true, not because of the worldly advantage that accrues from the belief.[10]

Bergin writes as though it would be unproblematic to achieve unanimity on the empirical relationships between the values people endorse and the associated levels of psychopathology. Given the complexities of the variables involved and the practical difficulties in constructing adequate experimental controls, scientific investigation of the link between values and psychological well-being is fraught with methodological difficulties. In fact, the correlational studies conducted to date on religion and mental health have yielded equivocal and confusing findings (Gartner, Larson, & Allen, 1991).

The ambiguity in the relationship between religious values and mental health is further illustrated by the views of Albert Ellis, a pundit who would endorse Bergin's view of psychotherapy as an educational enterprise directed at the client's entire worldview, including her values. For Ellis, therapy is an educational process in which certain values are aggressively championed. Ellis also has adopted Bergin's criterion for evaluating values, that is, their causal relation to mental health and happiness. Although these two theorists agree on the value-laden nature of therapy and on what standards and methods should be used to determine the "soundness" of values, they are in disagreement on the question of which particular values scientific findings have bolstered. Ellis (1983, p. 8), with great conviction and vigor, has prosecuted a polemic *against* religious belief: "Religiosity is, on almost every conceivable count, opposed to the normal goals of mental health. Instead, it encourages masochism, other-directedness, social withdrawal, intolerance, refusal to accept ambiguity and uncertainty, unscientific thinking, needless inhibition, lack of self-acceptance, and reluctance to acknowledge and deal adequately with reality." If these great differences in interpretation of the data are any indication, consensus on the psychological effects of value systems is not likely.

The Evolutionary Perspective

Another approach that acknowledges the evaluative aspects inherent in psychotherapy and psychodiagnostic classification is found in the writings of Wakefield (1992, 1993). Using a formulation analogous to that of Edwards (1982), Wakefield suggests that the category of mental illnesses subsumes both descriptive *and* evaluative dimensions, partakes of both science and values. His is a dual-component model of psychopathology that conceptualizes mental illness as "harmful dysfunction," wherein "harmful" refers to value judgments and "dysfunction" refers to matters of fact. Wakefield tells us that to conclude that a circumstance is "harmful" is to render a judgment about its desirability rather than its factual status. Our criteria for judging harm or desirability are socially constructed, subjective, and variable across societies and over historical time. According to Wakefield, the concept of "dysfunction" has to do with the objective, value-neutral description of natural kinds, that is, a "failure of a mechanism in the person to perform a natural function for which the mechanism was designed by natural selection" (1993, p. 165). Panic disorder, conceived as a "misfiring" of the fight-or-flight warning system under conditions where no objectively harmful threat is present, is an example of a disorder conceptualized as a dysfunctional mechanism, one taken from the current *Diagnostic and Statistical Manual of the American Psychiatric Association (DSM-IV)*. In Wakefield's view, we can rely on the objective evidence of evolutionary psychobiology and its various criteria of adaptive fitness to determine the natural and proper functioning of the human organism.

In their critique of Wakefield's work, Lilienfeld and Marino (1995) persuasively argue that appealing to evolutionary adaptation for the criteria of mental illness is ultimately futile. The various forms of psychopathology cannot be adequately explained by any set of mechanisms that are indubitable adaptations preserved by natural selection, either performing or not performing the functions for which they were "designed." From the perspective of evolutionary biology, our present psychic machinery comprises not only adaptations but also *exaptations* and *spandrels*. It is only adaptations that could be playing the roles for which they were designed by natural selection. Exaptations are features that subsequently play a role for which they were not originally designed. For example, it is likely that feathers originally evolved as insulation and served that function before being co-opted to facilitate flight. Spandrels are "unintended" by-products of the adaptive process that had no initial adaptive utility but later came to be useful to a species (Gould, 1996). For example, the taste for poetry and the capacity for philosophical reflection have, we assume, little direct connection with the functions their correlated adaptations originally served.

Lilienfeld and Marino conclude, as did Sedgwick, that mental disorder is a "nonscientific concept lacking clearcut natural boundaries" (1995, p. 417). They reach this conclusion largely because all efforts to date have failed to identify, in nature, objective features that are common elements underlying the various mental disorders described in the DSM. Nor do there appear to be distinct natural boundaries that unambiguously divide mental illness from other patterns of cognition, affect, and behavior. What seems to characterize mental disorders, most essentially, is a kind of loose categorical coherence (see Rosch, 1973) and a high degree of public consensus on their undesirability.

These last points, or any others made in this chapter, do not mean that there cannot be a science of psychopathology or an applied science of psychotherapy. There are and will be such sciences. What is in question is the nature of such sciences and to what range of human activity they should be applied, either as metaphor or as technology. To consider that issue without falling into conceptual muddles, we must examine our concept of objectivity and its relation to the value-laden nature of social phenomena and, indeed, to all human practices, including science.

Whither Objectivity?

People who worry about the evaluative status of mental health labels often assume that facts and values are categorically separate and that, to the extent that psychotherapy and psychodiagnosis are about social norms or evaluative criteria, these practices are unscientific. Some years ago most philosophers would have agreed. G. E. Moore (1903/1966) coined the term *naturalistic fallacy* to describe the unsound reasoning involved when we attempt to derive value judgments from matters of fact. The logical positivists (Ayer, 1946) separated fact and value, relegating the latter to the realm of unverifiable subjectivity. Philosophers these days, however, are less certain than those of the mid-twentieth century that fact and value always can be differentiated unproblematically.

There have been questions raised about whether any science, even a paradigmatic endeavor such as physics, is value-free. Merton (1973) suggested that the ease and frequency with which scientists, as contrasted with other scholars, reach agreement on findings results from shared norms that regulate conduct within the scientific community. According to this view, science achieves stable patterns of consensus because scientists adhere to a common system of values that includes universalism, communalism, disinterestedness, and organized skepticism. Advancing a similar view, Rorty (1991) reminds us that the values of science and those of democracy—namely, openness, egalitarianism, and unconstrained discourse—overlap and converge historically. Laudan (1984) contends that science is predicated on an axiology or set of cognitive values. These values include coherence, simplicity, and predictive fertility. The values are not themselves products of scientific research but are action-orienting norms, established a priori. Putnam (1981) argues that values are presupposed by the practices of scientific inquiry and by our conception of rationality itself, which we in turn rely on to determine "what is and what is not a fact" (p. 128). What we call facts are predicated on categories of understanding that derive from our practical needs and objectives. In the absence of the values associated with our practices, we could not perceptually organize the world into objects, things, and events, the kinds of experiential entities that we take as self-evident "facts": "Without the cognitive values of coherence, simplicity, and instrumental efficacy, we have no world and no facts, not even facts about what is so *relative* to what, for those are in the same boat with all other facts. And these cognitive values are arbitrary considered as anything but a part of a holistic conception of human flourishing" (Putnam, 1981, p. 136). Our picture of the empirical world is constituted by values. For Putnam, both science and ethics, facts and values, are inevitably bound up in human practices and guided by socially instantiated ideals that reflect what we believe to be good or worthwhile.

The compatibility of science and values, and a holism with regard to all forms of inquiry, including natural science, social science, and ethics, are assumed by writers such as Dewey (1938) and his neopragmatist admirers Putnam and Rorty. These thinkers espouse not the position that science and ethics are interchangeable but rather the view that both ethical and scientific inquiry are forms of reflective thinking orchestrated within a social context and directed toward human aims. Scientific and moral belief systems are, for Dewey, forms of coping with the practical exigencies of everyday life. In Dewey's view, both science and ethics ideally should "exhibit free intelligence operating in the best manner available at a given time" (1938, p. 535).

Contemporary empirical research suggests that no vocabulary for describing human beings could be cleansed of its evaluative dimension. Human processes of perception and cognition seemingly do not occur without some element of evaluation (Bargh, 1995), even when the stimuli involved are ostensibly unvalenced. We "like" and "dislike," we evaluate differentially, such meaningless, made-up words as *gumok* or *taleer*. In our everyday descriptions, the evaluative dimension is preeminent, dwarfing and subsuming other semantic dimensions (Osgood, Suci, & Tannenbaum, 1957; Kim & Rosenberg, 1980). Our ordinary language is simultaneously descriptive and evaluative, but so too are the lexicons of the clinical and social sciences. If we refer to an individual as "obnoxious" or "considerate," we describe her, but we also offer an evaluation (Peabody, 1967; Putnam, 1981). The dual functions of description and evaluation are inherent, as well, in such "scientific" terms as *borderline personality* and *prosocial behavior*. This duality of description is not a matter of two distinct classes of things being referred to, as Wakefield would have it, but rather an interpenetration of the categories of fact and value, such that a single description is, at once and holistically, both factual and evaluative.

Many human endeavors are concurrently explanatory and evaluative. Psychotherapy and psychodiagnosis are such activities. So are medical treatment and diagnosis. The value structure of medicine, however, is less salient to us and also less a matter of controversy than are the normative underpinnings of psychotherapy. The values underlying the goal of physical health (that is, the avoidance of pain, physical incapacity, and death) are so simple, so basic, and so widely agreed upon that they recede far into the background, so far that medical objectives seem not to involve value judgments at all. The connection between somatic medicine and values is clearest at the beginning and end of life, as the debates on abortion and euthanasia attest. The value-laden and sometimes arbitrary nature of medical decisions, however, will become more apparent if the current trend of controlling access to health care services continues. Physicians and managed health care companies are already beginning to ponder the trade-offs between comfort and health risk, on the one hand, and costs of treatment, on the other.

As we saw in Chapter Two, the findings and theories that underlie the mental health professions intertwine with cultural values in ways that are extensive, complex, and integral. Indeed, human values and the phenomena associated with them, such as motivation, emotion, and interpersonal relations, are the very subject matter of psychology and psychiatry. One of the social functions of these fields is that of providing us with cognitive, emotional, and behavioral norms. These fields speak directly to us on the questions of who we are and what kind of life should be acceptable to us. There is virtually no aspect of the human self-concept that they do not study and influence. It is, therefore, unsurprising that the mental health professions and the disciplines on which they are based cannot avoid the imprecision and lack of consensus that ensue when what is at stake are those self-referential and self-defining issues that are so important to human beings and on which they disagree so often and so vehemently.

Chapter Four

Psychotherapy as Humanism

Thus far we have seen how psychotherapy and its related theories function culturally as systems of belief and as means of social regulation. Another perspective on psychotherapy, explored in the preceding chapter, construes it as an applied science of behavior change. From yet another vantage point, that of the present chapter, psychotherapy can be viewed as a contemporary form of an ancient and perennial Western practice, that of self-examination. Self-exploration most often has been associated with the arts and humanities, rather than the sciences. When it is employed as a vehicle for self-examination, psychotherapy can be conceived, not as a science or a behavioral technology but as a set of humanistic practices aimed at self-discovery and self-realization.

For over two thousand years, within various cultural precincts of the Western tradition, self-knowledge and self-understanding have been considered essential components of human excellence. Knowledge of oneself has tended to mean different things in different eras and in different civilizations. Self-examination has served diverse purposes, ranging from civic solidarity to religious piety to personal growth and happiness.

In the ancient world, self-understanding was sought in the service of communal and religious purposes. Private life was subordinate to action in the public realm. The notion of an individual self as something unique and intrinsically valuable, knowledge of which is inherently worthwhile, did not appear until the modern era (Baumeister, 1986; Taylor, 1989).

Individualism and the prerogatives of individual self-fulfillment were established during the philosophical and political upheavals of the eighteenth century. With the advent of rights to life, liberty, and the pursuit of happiness, self-knowledge came to be regarded as an indispensable component of self-realization. For Lionel Trilling (1971) the shift from premodern to modern views of the person is associated with the movement from an ethic of "sincerity," or congruence between inner experience and public portrayal, toward an ethic of "authenticity," wherein the aim is that of being "true," not to others but rather to one's own inner being, desires, and proclivities. Private life comes to assume a priority over one's social roles and obligations.

The psychotherapists who paved the way for what would later be called "humanistic psychology," Carl Jung, Karen Horney, and Eric Fromm, wholeheartedly endorsed a value system that emphasized, above all, being true to oneself. Pursuit of the "ethic of self-realization" (Horney, 1950) dictated seeking, with the aid of therapy, the "healthy," "non-neurotic" self that frequently is suppressed, distorted, and obscured by neurotic defenses and by pathological idealized self-images. The exploration, comprehension, and expression of an inner or "true" self, pursuant to the goal of self-realization or self-actualization, became the central project of those forms of psychotherapy that were grounded in neither behaviorism nor psychoanalysis and that eschewed the scientific pretensions so important to both.

Knowing Oneself

Approaches to psychotherapy that emphasize self-exploration and self-discovery are ideologically modern, in that they are predicated on the Western, individualistic conception of selfhood that regards the inner self as the essence of the person. Yet these forms of therapy have roots in religious and philosophical practices that antedate the modern view of selfhood. Efforts to discover and unfetter what is good and true within the person have been part of the human landscape for many centuries.

Greco-Roman Precursors

The Greeks were under the injunction of Apollo as transmitted through the Delphic oracle: "Know thyself." They were instructed further by Socrates that the unexamined life was not worth living. In Plato's *Phaedrus*, Socrates states that he cares only about knowing himself, other pursuits being "laughable" in the absence of self-knowledge. According to the classicist Dihle (1982), the message contained in the histories of Herodotus and the tragedies of Sophocles is that knowledge of oneself and, especially, of one's shortcomings is the necessary foundation for freedom of moral choice. Both Plato and Aristotle believed that a deep and thoroughgoing understanding of oneself was indispensable to a virtuous life (Flanagan, 1991). This kind of knowledge of oneself is a component of *sophrosyne*, literally "moral sanity." The term was used by the Greeks to refer to self-knowledge that is expressed in action (North, 1966). *Sophrosyne* is that state that is opposite to madness.[11] An adequate synonym from the contemporary lexicon would be either "maturity" or, perhaps, "emotional intelligence."

For the Greeks, the pursuit of self-knowledge was a singular psychological activity always to be related to the exploration of human nature in general. To examine an individual life was to learn about all lives and the generalities that apply to them, especially those having to do with the limits of human power and ambition (Jaeger, 1939). Self-knowledge was pursued for the sake of other ends that were believed to transcend self-interest: moral excellence, rationality, or social harmony. The modern concept of self-understanding, in which it is viewed as an end in itself had no place within the Greek worldview.

The Greek tradition of self-examination was preserved and extended by philosophers of the Hellenistic period. A common thread between the Stoics and the Epicureans was their conception of philosophy as the practical art of analyzing and coping with the concerns of everyday life. Martha Nussbaum's recent book (1994) has argued effectively that much of Hellenistic philosophy is viewed properly as "therapeutic" in its aims and methods. Within these schools the philosopher was as much a teacher of living skills and healer of souls as a discoverer of truth (Albert, Denise, & Peterfreund, 1980). Both Epicureanism and Stoicism assume that in order to achieve psychic prosperity, the individual must engage in searching self-scrutiny. For these thinkers, happiness and tranquility require a foundation of self-knowledge. The philosopher is a teacher whose pedagogy "is manifold, complex, and personal. The teacher's job requires subtle psychological interaction at a deep level, which grapples with whatever memories, wishes, fears, and habits influence the pupil. . . . The teacher is a doctor—but a doctor who leads the patient in an exacting exploration of her own insides" (Nussbaum, 1994, p. 328).

Gnosis

It was Augustine who provided the first systematic, recorded attempt to delve introspectively into one's private experience as a means for the discovery of important truths. His *Confessions* is the first autobiography of an inner life. In a sense, he established the intellectual importance of subjectivity as well as the fecundity of deep self-exploration: "Men go to gape at mountain peaks, at the boundless tides of the sea, the broad sweep of rivers, the encircling ocean and the motions of the stars: and yet they leave themselves unnoticed; they do not marvel at themselves" (Augustine, 1992, p. 72).

Augustine did marvel at himself. For him the body and the outer world, the material world, were to be contrasted with the subjective world, identified with mind, soul, and spirituality. The possession of an inner life was what distinguished humans from animals, and marked their elevation. For Augustine, the answers to most important questions are to be found through self-scrutiny. "Do not go outward," he directs us. "Return within yourself. In the inward man dwells truth" (cited in Taylor, 1989, p. 129).

Gnosticism, the doctrines of early sects (second to fourth centuries A.D.) that combined Platonism and Christianity, contrasted the evil material world with the goodness of the spiritual world (Pagels, 1979). *Gnosis*, or knowledge that grants salvation, is identified with the divinity of the inner self. Self-exploration becomes the path away from the evil of the world toward the divine world of the psyche or spirit. Gnosticism entails "a 'passionate subjectivity' which counts the world well lost for the sake of self-discovery, . . . recognition of the divine element which constitutes the true self" (Grant, 1959, p. 10).

Friedman (1978) has described how views derived from Gnosticism pervade the work of the first humanistic psychologist, Carl Jung. Jung introduced the concept of "self-actualization" into the vernacular of the mental health professions. He is the first great contributor who could be said to have placed decided emphasis on "growth" or "potential," as opposed to "illness" or "pathology": " 'Growth' is the objective activity of the psyche, which, independently of conscious volition, is trying to speak to the conscious mind through the inner voice and lead . . . [it] toward wholeness . . . the growth of personality, the full realization of the life-will that is born with the individual" (Friedman, 1978, p. 157).

In Jung's view there is no essential difference between the modern person's relation to the inner self and the Augustinian or Gnostic sense of connection with the manifestations of God within oneself. Jung's deification of the self is explicit in his writings: "The goal of psychological, as of biological, development is self-realization, or individuation. But since man knows himself only as an ego, and the self, as a totality, is indescribable and indistinguishable from a God-image, self-realization—to put it in religious or metaphysical terms—*amounts to God's incarnation*" (Jung, 1958, p. 157).

The passionate subjectivity and belief in the sacral character of the inner life that have their origins in the early Christian world resurfaced and found expression in another movement that foreshadowed humanistic psychotherapy—Romanticism.

Romanticism

The rudiments of the contemporary enterprise that is humanistic psychology are recognizable in the writings of Rousseau, Herder, Byron, and Goethe (Randall, 1926; Taylor, 1975). It was Rousseau (1762/1911) who famously valorized the "noble savage" as the personification of the innocent purity of nature, uncorrupted by civilization. Human beings are by nature good. Evil is the product of human society. Rousseau's basic premise is preserved in the humanistic psychology of Rogers, Maslow, and Perls, wherein, contra Freud, the essence of human nature is not a bestiality, destructiveness, nor lasciviousness that needs to be controlled, diverted, and sublimated, but rather a salubrious innocence that should be preserved, fostered, and, ultimately, liberated.

One perspective on the Romantic movement is to view it as an attempted corrective to the objectified, rationalist philosophical anthropology that emerged from the Enlightenment. The Romantics were uneasy about science, fearing that its modes of description and analysis might come to dominate all intellectual activity, thereby rendering it sterile and lifeless. If Newton is the prototypical hero of the Enlightenment, Byron personifies the Romantic era. Romanticism counters thinking with feeling, utility with beauty, logic with intuition, science with art, convention with rebellion. Byron boldly declares that the Tree of Knowledge does not illumine human existence. Passion, especially intense passion, is a life compass superior to that of reason: "Romanticism makes the emancipated feelings the sovereign legislator for each man and for all mankind; directly applies these feelings to the complicated circumstances of the daily life resolving the riddles of tangled interest by reference to the command of love and the dictate of will" (Nelson, 1975, p. 154).

Contemporary Humanistic Psychology

In accord with the Romantic temper, humanistic psychology holds that each of us can be an artist whose masterwork is her own self-realization. We begin life not as undifferentiated pools of depraved primal urges, pace Freud, but as Rousseau's noble primitives. The grace, joy, and innocence of childhood give way to the robotic, intellectualized, conforming modes of other-directedness as we lose touch with those inner sources of emotional fecundity.

Humanistic psychology (Maslow, 1968; Rogers, 1961; Perls, 1969) and the associated human potential movement are perhaps best thought of as a Romantic, Dionysian counterpoint to the classical, Apollonian sensibilities of both psychoanalysis and behaviorism. Humanistic psychotherapy has emphasized the cultivation of emotional sensitivity and expressiveness. Humanistic psychologists venerate spontaneity, creativity, authenticity, and experiential intensity. The Apollonian values of moderation, restraint, order, reason, and sobriety often are regarded by humanists as spiritual straitjackets placed on the psyche by a society whose strictures are inimical to the self-actualizing propensities possessed by all but thwarted in most. The project of humanistic psychotherapy is to help the individual restore contact with emotions, feelings, and sensations, and to enable that inner experience to be channeled into behavior without distortion or censorship. Self-awareness and self-expression become the agents of our redemption from the benumbing influences of contemporary existence. In place of the balance, self-control, and rationality sought by psychoanalysis and behavioral approaches alike, the humanistic alternatives offer a celebration of the passions, a cultivation of sensitivity to experience, and the development of spontaneity and emotionality.

Self-knowledge is vital to the program of humanistic psychology. Yet what passes for self-understanding in the writings of Perls, Maslow, and Rogers would not have been recognizable to the Greeks who followed the Delphic prescription to achieve self-knowledge. Fritz Perls often stated that a goal of Gestalt therapy was to help clients "lose their minds and come to their senses" (Levitsky & Perls, 1970, p. 143). Carl Rogers (1961, 1980) wrote extensively about the importance of being "in touch" with one's feelings. For the humanistic psychologist, cognitive processes represent only a fraction of the experience that can be grasped by a fully functioning human being. Humanistic psychology designates emotional experience, bodily sensations, and nonverbal behavior as critical domains that must be encompassed in order to achieve a comprehensive understanding of self.

In humanistic psychology, greater self-understanding means greater awareness of and sensitivity to one's experience. Experience is defined broadly to include what Arnold Lazarus (1981) would term multiple "psychological modalities": sensation, affect, imagery, and behavior, in addition to cognition. Humanistic psychotherapy is, fundamentally, training in the registration and appreciation of those features of experience given short shrift by therapies that emphasize an approach to living more influenced by intellectual considerations (for example, psychoanalysis and cognitive therapy). It therefore inevitably occupies that cultural territory wherein reside artists, writers, and other explorers of subjectivity who yearn to roam free over the broad landscape of possible human experience.

Humanistic psychology emerged during the 1940s and 1950s as a deliberate effort to counteract the scientism of both behaviorism and psychoanalysis. Humanistic psychologists believed that the scientific pretensions of the two preeminent schools of psychology had produced therapeutic ideologies that were excessively deterministic and reductionistic. What was needed, according to the founders of the so-called Third Force in psychology, was an alternative framework, one that allowed the study of human beings but did not, through abstraction or dissection, eliminate from its subject matter those qualities that are most distinctively human.

Humanistic psychologists were not the first students of human conduct to turn to the arts and humanities for methods and for inspiration. Philosophers in nineteenth-century Germany had wrestled with many of the same concerns. Out of those efforts hermeneutic philosophy arose.

Hermeneutics

Hermeneutics is a broad-based intellectual movement that has sought to counteract the dominance of scientific modes of thinking within modern culture. Hermeneuticists such as Charles Taylor and Clifford Geertz have been intent on criticizing positivistic approaches to the social sciences and on advocating various methodological alternatives. Jürgen Habermas has concerned himself with, among other things, the development of a critical theory of society that seeks to identify the implicit ideological underpinnings of both the natural and social sciences. Still others, such as Martin Heidegger and Hans-Georg Gadamer, have disdained any direct attempt to influence scientific practice but have sought to contextualize scientific activity by analyzing its relations with other forms of understanding. In so doing, they have subjected to critique the positivist worldview that takes natural science and mathematics as the standards by which all knowledge claims must be evaluated. The common threads that unite these otherwise diverse hermeneutic positions are a humanistic opposition to scientism and positivism, and an attempt to supply philosophical, cultural, and methodological correctives to objectivism, mechanism, and technicism—the perspectives that have dominated the social sciences and mental health professions.

Recently, the discussion of hermeneutic views has become widespread in the social sciences and the humanities. Clinical psychology, psychiatry, and psychoanalysis have begun to feel the impact as their predominant methods, theories, and philosophical underpinnings have come under hermeneutically inspired criticism. In the pages that follow I provide a brief overview of hermeneutics. My aim, in this and subsequent chapters, is to emphasize those aspects of hermeneutic thought that suggest motifs which may foster critical analysis and expansion of the applied science model of psychotherapy.

The Circle of Interpretation

Consider the following lines of a celebrated poem:

> Full many a gem of purest ray serene
> The dark unfathom'd caves of ocean bear.

What is being communicated here? Are we to take the sentence literally, or is the meaning figurative? The lines that follow in the poem serve to clarify the meaning:

> Full many a gem of purest ray serene
> The dark unfathom'd caves of ocean bear:
> Full many a flower is born to blush unseen,
> And waste its sweetness on the desert air.

With additional components available we begin to see better the character of the whole. But also the meaning of the particular lines we originally examined is elucidated. We understand an attitude or tone of lamentation and loss directed toward the beauty that lies in "unfathomed" repositories and is, consequently, subject to "waste."

Another verse of the poem both illuminates the parts we have already seen and begins to give us a better and more complete sense of the whole:

> The boast of heraldry, the pomp of pow'r,
> All that beauty, all that wealth e're gave,
> Awaits alike th' inevitable hour:
> The paths of glory lead but to the grave.

Voila! More is revealed and we see that this is a poem not of plant life and mineralogy but about the fortuitousness and finitude of human existence. Gems and flowers are metaphors for lives that "blush unseen," for those "mute" and "inglorious" Miltons that are among the subjects of Thomas Gray's "Elegy Written in a Country Churchyard."[12] We need the whole in order to make sense of its parts and to understand what these parts signify in this particular poetic context. But also clearly what we here are calling the context (the whole poem) is made up of and determined by its parts.

What we have traversed in this exercise is the celebrated hermeneutic circle, as it was formulated by Schleiermacher (1819/1985). The hermeneutic circle describes both the actual process and the a priori structure of linguistic understanding. When we interpret a literary work, for example, our process of understanding is a continual movement back and forth between whole and part. Our knowledge of the whole results from a grasp of the meanings of its component parts, but the interpretation of the parts relies on some overall sense of the whole within which the parts are contextualized.

Hermeneutics had its origin in the interpretation of Biblical texts (Palmer, 1969). With the advent of the Reformation came the revisionist view that the scriptures were possessed of a literary completeness that allowed for their interpretation independent of the offices and tradition of the church. Biblical exegesis was an art that potentially could be practiced by anyone with adequate interpretive skills. Biblical scholars began to ask the question, How are we to decide what it is that a particular passage of text conveys? Their answers to that question became the field of biblical hermeneutics. Subsequently, this identification, explication, and codification of interpretive techniques and principles found a wider range of application to such secular topics as jurisprudence and the deciphering of classical works. By the beginning of the nineteenth century, hermeneutics had been broadened so as to address any domain in which signification was nebulous (Woolfolk, Sass, & Messer, 1988).

Dilthey and the Geisteswissenschaften

In the writings of Wilhelm Dilthey (1976, 1989) hermeneutics was appropriated as a method for the then nascent human sciences, the Geisteswissenschaften.[13] Dilthey's ideas emerged in the intellectual context of late-nineteenth-century Germany. There the social and behavioral sciences, as we recognize them in contemporary Anglo-American universities, existed only in inchoate form. The rudiments of the specialized disciplines of psychology, economics, anthropology, sociology, history, and linguistics were admixed, in various proportions, within the work of generalists. There was great agreement that the study of human beings represented an exciting new intellectual frontier, but there was also much debate over just what methods and assumptions would yield the most comprehensive and productive science of human life.

One viewpoint on how to study persons was positivism. Positivism began with Thomas Hobbes (1651/1962), who envisioned a deterministic science of human life, modeled on physics, comprising social and psychological "laws" from which precise predictions of behavior could be made. Dilthey's predecessor and intellectual foil, Auguste Comte, advocated a unified, hierarchical scientific system in which the "positive" (physical) sciences served as the foundation for the biological sciences, which, in turn, would be the foundation for sociology (Makkreel, 1975). Comte, who coined the term *positivism*, believed that psychology, construed as the study of mental processes, was superfluous to the study of human conduct—which he believed could be accounted for satisfactorily by biology and sociology. Another positivist writer whose work gave impetus to Dilthey's thinking was John Stuart Mill (1843/1973). Though Mill did not subscribe to Comte's elimination of psychology from the human sciences, he held the mechanistic view that the structures of mental life are best accounted for by the essentially passive processes of sensation and association, through which elemental building blocks of experience accumulate and develop into more complex psychological structures. Dilthey came to reject both Comte's behaviorism and Mill's associationist psychology. And whereas positivists wished to make the study of human beings special instances of an overarching, methodologically homogeneous science, Dilthey concluded that a science of human beings should employ methods and concepts unlike those of physics and chemistry.

Dilthey believed the positivist program for the human sciences to be misguided because it failed to take into account what he regarded as essential qualitative differences between human beings and inanimate objects. For him what is fundamental to the human realm and what has no analog in the physical sphere is what he termed "lived experience" *(Erlebnis)*. He writes: "systems of culture, commerce, law, religion, art and scholarship and the outer organization of society in family, community, church and state originated from the living context of the human mind and, ultimately, can only be understood through it" (1976, p. 90). Dilthey argued that there is no transcendental framework outside of human experience within which human action can be rendered in purely objective terms. Each human life is ineluctably enmeshed in a web of meaning. The meanings we attach to our beliefs and behavior are integral to them. From a Diltheyian point of view, such metatheories as behaviorism, which seek to emulate the physical sciences by ruling out-of-bounds any meanings or purposes that are associated with behavior, are wrongheaded, because they eliminate the very essence of that which they seek to render and explain. Dilthey adopted from the German historiographer J. G. Droysen the distinction between explanation *(Erklaren)* and understanding *(Verstehen)*.

For Dilthey, *explanation* is a purely intellectual process that involves comprehending specific, objective phenomena under general laws. In explanation the aim is always to give an account of a particular individual phenomenon in terms of some more general explanatory principle. Dilthey contended that in the natural sciences, explanation is entirely sufficient to map the causal relations among the entities these disciplines study. Because the phenomena investigated in the natural sciences are not the products or expressions of psychic life, there is no need to recover the mental impetus that gave rise to them.

In contradistinction, *understanding* concerns itself not with behavior per se, abstracted from the significance it has for the persons who produce it, but rather with human action, conceived as meaningful, purpose-laden expressions of mental life. For Dilthey, as it would be for Max Weber and Alfred Schutz, basic social facts are not the external mechanical motions of human bodies but the underlying significance of these acts for the actors. Whereas the physical sciences require no cognitive form other than explanation, in the human studies the kind of knowledge given by explanation is not sufficient.

In Anglo-American circles (Danto, 1968; Nagel, 1961) the concept of *Verstehen* has been the subject of much misconstrual. It has been regarded as the equivalent of an "empathic understanding" that requires a transposition of the consciousness of the social scientist into the subjective awareness of the individual whose actions are to be explained. Thus if I wish to understand why John Wilkes Booth shot Abraham Lincoln, so the stereotype of *Verstehen* goes, I must see the world through Booth's eyes by intuitively grasping his emotional and cognitive processes, by feeling as he felt. The stereotype of *Verstehen* suggests that because knowledge of persons consists in inspection of their inner worlds, then self-knowledge analogously would be best generated through introspection. To the tough-minded empirical behavioral scientist, *Verstehen*-based approaches seem loose and almost literary, requiring quasi-clairvoyant forays out of the sphere of publicly observable events and onto the slippery slopes of human subjectivity.

This commonly held view of *Verstehen*, however, does not do justice to the complexities of the interpretive methods of Dilthey, or even of his forerunner, Schleiermacher.[14] *Verstehen* involves what Dilthey termed "re-experiencing" (*Nacherleben*). But this term referred not to empathic understanding (which is translated better in German as *Einfühlen*) but rather to an interpretive reconstruction of the total person-environment field.[15]

For Dilthey the hermeneutics of human action involves interpreting the relations among lived experience (*Erlebnis*), expression (*Ausdruck*), and understanding (*Verstehen*). Expressions refer to explicit, observable products of human subjectivity. Expressions can be the specific actions of individuals (such as my typing this sentence on my word processor) or the outcomes of those actions (for example, the sentence itself). Expressions also can refer to complex products of culture, such as a language or a system of laws. Expressions are "objectifications" of the subjective meanings and intentions that reside in the domain of *Erlebnis*. The knowledge of lived experience that is the goal of the *Geisteswissenschaften* can be achieved only indirectly, through interpreting and understanding the objectifications of life.

For Dilthey, mental life gives rise to expressions that are in turn understood by other minds. The understanding of social and psychological reality that is achieved through interpretation of public events is analogous to textual interpretation. The behavior of another is a text-analog that must be comprehended and elucidated by the interpreter. This kind of hermeneutic activity does not involve grasping the mind of another through an empathic fusion with another individual's phenomenal world. The aim is to understand the other more completely than that person can understand herself. This superior understanding is achieved through an assimilation of the complete sociohistorical reality that provides the context of any particular piece of behavior. The interpreter has multiple perspectives that are not available to the actor at the time of action. The interpreter can understand the relation of an action to a history of past behavior, to influential factors outside the actor's awareness, and to aspects of the broader sociocultural world of which the actor is a part.

Dilthey's work was the springboard and inspiration for many developments in the social sciences and in philosophy. His work directly influenced Weber's sociology and the philosophy of Husserl and Heidegger. We see his influence also in Gadamer's writings, in phenomenological sociology, various forms of existentialism, and in contemporary cognitive psychology. With Dilthey, hermeneutics becomes a humanistic model for the study of human behavior, one that attempts to emphasize qualitative, subjective, and idiographic methods versus quantitative, objective, and nomothetic approaches. Hermeneutics champions the values, sensibilities, and practices of the humanities in the study of human beings. Historically, hermeneutics and related views have served as counterweights to the scientism of mainstream social science.

Shortly, I will describe a "hermeneutic" conception of psychoanalysis that is grounded on distinctions first drawn by Dilthey. Hermeneutics came to be regarded as an attractive foundation for psychoanalysis by thinkers who were persuaded that psychotherapy is not a straightforward applied science. But we are getting ahead of ourselves. Before hermeneutics became a framework for therapy, it was developed in highly abstract philosophical ways by Heidegger and Gadamer.

Philosophical Hermeneutics

In the philosophy of Heidegger (1927/1962) there emerges a perspective on science that later was developed by his student Gadamer. As this view would have it, science is not the fundamental paradigmatic form of thinking but rather is one variation in thought that possesses unique advantages with respect to certain purposes and certain contexts of inquiry. Heidegger departed from those philosophers, such as Descartes, Hume, and Kant, who, writing in the wake of the scientific revolution, saw science as fundamental. They viewed it as the signal, bedrock form of thought that could provide methods and models to serve as the foundation for all intellectual endeavors.

One aim of Gadamerian hermeneutic philosophy is the intellectual rehabilitation of those cultural forms (art, ethics, literature) whose claims to produce valid knowledge, as opposed to mere opinion, are undermined by the positivist criteria of contemporary scientific culture. According to Gadamer (1975b, p. 316), hermeneutics serves to "defend practical and political reason against the domination of technology based on science. That is the point of philosophical hermeneutics. It corrects the peculiar falsehood of modern consciousness: the idolatry of scientific method and of the anonymous authority of the sciences."

For both Heidegger and Gadamer, science is not the unique province of truth. Science is only one path to truth, a pathway whose taking can obscure a broader, deeper, more primordial notion of truth upon which the scientific conception of truth is parasitic. According to Gadamer, truth is discovered not only in science but in the humanities and arts as well. Gadamer's concept of truth differs in important ways from the correspondence view of truth—in which truth is a property of mental or linguistic representations that either do or do not "match" the world as it is. The correspondence view of truth assumes that representation can be separated from reality and subsequently compared with it via some objective and disinterested procedure.

Gadamer argues that there is "truth" in art that the correspondence model cannot describe or comprehend. This is because the actuality or reality of a work of art cannot be separated, epistemologically speaking, from how it is understood. For example, within the performing arts many different valid presentations can represent a single work of art. There are many different productions of *Hamlet*, each of which emphasizes and reveals different aspects of the play. Yet in each case, *Hamlet*, one unity or structure, is represented. Just as every production of *Hamlet* may be distinctive, every reading of a great novel also may be unique, yielding diverse and incompatible interpretations. Gadamer's point here is *not* the rather obvious observation about human cognition: that what we comprehend is a function not only of the stimulus but also of the cognitive factors that structure and constitute experience. Gadamer's point is ontological rather than epistemological or psychological. He contends that the very *being* of the work of art and the reality it represents, that is, its truth, emerge *only* as interpreted by human beings. The content of art does not exist independent of human understanding and evaluation, and cannot be established independent of the act of interpretation.

What we see or fail to see in a text is partly a product of our own sociocultural horizon. The content a text has for us results from the "fusion" of our horizon of understanding with that of the text. This integration of what matters to us with what is represented by the text can be thought of as occurring in a field of understanding that comprises both subject and object, reader and text. The message of the text, its truth, ontologically speaking, is neither on the pages of the text nor in the head of the reader, but rather in what is synthesized in the interaction between reader and what is read.

Let me try to concretize this rather abstract set of ideas with an illustration. From the perspective of today we are able to see racism and sexism in the historical and literary record of the past, whereas only decades ago the concepts of sexism and racism, in their present forms, were unavailable to interpreters. At those earlier times, one could not see some of what we are able to observe *now* through the lens of the present. Undoubtedly, future interpreters of our world will find in it social phenomena of which we cannot yet dream. Now an objectivist might argue that sexism and racism were present in past eras but were unobservable without present-day conceptual apparatus. A social constructionist might argue that sexism and racism (and all other social categories) are present after and only after the categories are socially constructed and adopted as interpretive tools. Gadamer's hermeneutic position is intermediate. It does not hold that social explanation involves the arbitrary imposition of socially constructed concepts. An external social reality that interpreters can access does exist, but that reality emerges only through interpretation and is delimited by the variety of constraints to which interpretation is subject.

Our understanding of any human situation is constrained and influenced not only by our interpretive categories but also by the concerns and purposes we bring to the act of understanding. For Gadamer there is a practical, moral dimension in both the humanities and the human sciences that binds them together as common sources of the particular kind of understanding of self and world that makes a difference in one's conduct. There is always an element of application to self and to one's own situation involved in hermeneutic understanding. Gadamer (1975a, p. 289) contends that this application of an interpretation to oneself is an integral and necessary aspect of understanding: "In order to understand, he [the interpreter] cannot disregard himself and the particular hermeneutic situation in which he exists. He must relate the text to this situation if he wants to understand at all."

Gadamer wishes to demonstrate that human being-in-the-world and especially human self-understanding are not detached, disinterested relations between a subjective mental apparatus and an objectified external world. For Gadamer, hermeneutic understanding is ultimately self-understanding. In understanding any expression of life, whether it be a piece of behavior or a work of art, we must relate our understanding to the horizon of meaning in which we exist, and hence to our understanding of ourselves. When we seek to understand a work of art or a historical text, of necessity we must interpret it in light of the constraints and motives characteristic of our particular sociohistorical situation. In interpreting the products of human life and relating those interpretations to our concrete historical situation, we open ourselves to the influence of those interpretations. In the fusion of horizons between interpreter and that which is interpreted, there is a codetermination of each.

Given that our understanding of ourselves and of other people is orchestrated within a field of practical, value-laden concepts, our understanding of the social world will have practical, action-orienting implications. Of course, any knowledge can have practical implications. But our understanding of social reality almost always speaks to us in a personally relevant way and says "This is life. This is your life. Given this knowledge about life and about your life, live accordingly."

Gadamer uses the example of the tragic play to illustrate the self-reflexive nature of hermeneutic understanding. In his formulation, Gadamer follows Aristotle (trans. 1961), who included the effect of a tragedy on its audience in his definition of the tragic. The spectator is both distressed and comforted by the great tragedies. There is a recognition of shared human helplessness before the force of events. This impotence in the face of destiny is true of the mightiest, wisest, and most virtuous of mortals. *Oedipus Rex*, *Three Sisters*, all tragedy, reveals the truth of human finitude, although this revelation may take different forms or have different implications given varying horizons of interpretation. We come away from such plays knowing better our place in the flow of life, perhaps wiser in our recognition and acceptance of the unfairness and uncertainty of existence. Great art leads to self-examination. Or to put it in Gadamerian terms, the understanding or meaning of great art includes and is inseparable from self-exploration: "The spectator recognizes himself and his own finite being in the face of the power of fate. . . . The tragic emotion is not a response to the tragic course of events as such or to the justice of the fate that overtakes the hero, but to the metaphysical order of being that is true for all. To see that 'this is how it is' is a kind of self-knowledge for the spectator" (Gadamer, 1975a, p. 117).

The tragic play, like any work of art, exercises a kind of normative authority over its spectators and makes claims on them to take seriously the relevance of the work for their own lives. In the face of knowledge of this sort derived from such sources, we may not only come to understand ourselves differently but also be moved to change ourselves. In this way art can be therapeutic, not in the sense of pursuing a particular ideal of health or virtue, but in the sense of offering a practical self- and world-analysis.

Our interest in Gadamer is not in whether he has answered or clarified the perennial questions of philosophy, but rather in his humanistic, hermeneutic analysis of understanding and interpretation, and in the potential applicability of that analysis to psychotherapy. In subsequent chapters I explore Gadamer's view that self-understanding inevitably involves practical and moral dimensions. In the following section I examine some attempts to use hermeneutic ideas to fashion a model of psychotherapy, in which it is conceived as an interpretive humanistic discipline.

Hermeneutics as a Model for Psychotherapy

Within psychotherapy, hermeneutic ideas have been embraced most enthusiastically in some psychoanalytic circles, where there has been a growing disaffection with mechanistic models of the psyche and with the conceptions of psychoanalytic psychotherapy as an objective scientific technology or research tool. Hermeneutic thought has supplied an alternative framework that conceives of psychoanalysis as an interpretive discipline grounded as much in the humanities as in the sciences.[16] Two hermeneutic philosophers, Jürgen Habermas and Paul Ricoeur, were most immediately responsible for influencing psychoanalysis in the direction of hermeneutics. Both writers developed their ideas during the course of philosophical explorations of Freud's ideas.

Habermas

The early writings of Habermas (1971) produced not only a hermeneutic reconceptualization of psychotherapy but also the novel view that the quest for knowledge that occurs in psychotherapy is a model of inquiry that can be applied fruitfully to a variety of intellectual disciplines. Habermas's work is an outgrowth of Critical Theory, a body of political philosophy and social criticism produced by members of the Frankfurt Institute of Social Research, established in 1923. The best known of these "Frankfurt School" thinkers were Max Horkheimer, Theodor Adorno, and Herbert Marcuse. The Frankfurt School advanced critical social theory as an alternative to the positivistic social science that purports to be value-free and politically neutral. Very much in the Marxist tradition, the aim of critical social theory is not only to understand the world but also to change it along democratic and egalitarian lines: "the [critical] theoretician and his specific object are seen as forming a dynamic unity with the oppressed class, so that his presentation of societal contradictions is not merely an expression of the concrete historical situation but also a force to stimulate change" (Horkheimer & Adorno, 1972, p. 215).

As were his Critical Theorist predecessors, Habermas is strongly influenced by psychoanalytic ideas. Critical social theorists had already used psychoanalytic ideas to extend the sociological and economic horizons of Marxist theory by adding to it a psychoanalytic psychology of the individual. For Habermas, however, it is the dialogic *form* of psychoanalytic therapy, the epistemic structure of the therapy process rather than the content of psychoanalytic theory, that is crucial. According to Habermas, in his invention of psychoanalysis Freud created not only a new discipline but a new category of discipline, one that yields a kind of knowledge different from that discovered by the sciences and the humanities.

For Habermas there is an inevitable and inextricable linkage between knowledge and its social origin and social function. Therefore, comprehending the relationship between a body of thought and its social context is essential to a complete understanding of the knowledge itself. One framework Habermas employs to characterize the sociocultural dimensions of knowledge is what he terms "cognitive interests." Cognitive interests describe the human concerns that underlie intellectual disciplines. Habermas contends that it is human motivation and values that determine much of the character of knowledge within various fields. What we study and how we study it will, to a great degree, emanate from the human interests and purposes that underlie any framework of inquiry.

The three primary cognitive interests Habermas enunciates are the *technical*, the *practical*, and the *emancipatory*. He provides a tripartite typology of knowledge containing three disciplinary categories, each corresponding to one of the cognitive interests. Thus the *empirical-analytic* disciplines (the natural sciences) are underlain by a technical interest directed toward control over nature. These sciences are characterized by quantification, general laws, prediction of natural phenomena, and highly refined and systematic empirical testing procedures. Unlike the natural sciences, the *historical-hermeneutic* sciences *(Geisteswissenschaften)* gain knowledge within a different methodological framework. Data are generated by the understanding of human meanings, not through the direct observation of neutral facts. The verification of lawlike hypotheses in the empirical-analytic sciences has its counterpart here in the interpretation of texts. Thus, hermeneutic procedures determine the validity of theories and propositions advanced within the human sciences. These disciplines are shaped by a practical interest that serves to clarify the conditions underlying communication and social interaction. Historical-hermeneutic sciences thus serve to promote intersubjective understanding, to establish those shared cultural meanings that are the prerequisites for social consensus on the practical dimensions of life. In his distinction between the empirical-analytic and historical-hermeneutic sciences, Habermas essentially recreates the typology of natural and human sciences found in Dilthey.

To Habermas, psychoanalysis represents an integration of aspects of both the empirical-analytic sciences and the historical-hermeneutic disciplines. As in the natural sciences, psychoanalysis traces causal connections, puts forward explanatory hypotheses, and tests them against empirical observation. But psychoanalysis is also clearly a form of hermeneutics, in that the reconstruction of the patient's past must ultimately rest not on direct observation of "brute data" but on the analyst's interpretation of events on which the patient already has conferred meaning. According to Habermas, the hermeneutic aims and methods of psychoanalysis differ from those of history or archeology. Historical-hermeneutic disciplines aim at a veridical reconstruction of the previous eras through an interpretation of meaning structures, by reading and deciphering the "texts" of history. This is one aim of psychoanalysis as well. But in addition to the objective of understanding, psychoanalysis also seeks transformation, the liberation of present capacities for action from the psychic fetters of the past. It therefore belongs in Habermas's scheme to a third sphere of intellectual activity, the *empirical-critical*. The empirical-critical sciences are guided by an *emancipatory* interest, one that serves the aims of human freedom and seeks the liberation of humankind from various forms of arbitrary control. Habermas also lists critical social theory among the empirical-critical sciences. When human capacities for self-determination are limited by sociological or political sources, Critical Theory, by providing social critique, instigates social correctives, functioning at the level of society as a *sociotherapy*, much as psychoanalysis operates as a psychotherapy at the level of the individual.

Freud had sought to conceptualize psychoanalysis in the causal language of the natural sciences, producing what sometimes is referred to as the *metapsychology*. The psychoanalytic metapsychology comprises the models of the psyche that describe its structure and function. The tripartite depiction of the psychic apparatus as being composed of id, ego, and super-ego and the relations of energy exchange among them is the foundation of the metapsychology. This energic, psychosexual, quasi-biological scheme is Freud's nineteenth-century mechanistic metaphor for the mind. According to Habermas, Freud was so seduced by nineteenth-century scientism that he fell prey to a "scientistic misunderstanding" of his own creation (psychoanalysis) and thereby obscured its true status as a "depth hermeneutic" that incorporates both explanation and understanding in facilitating processes of critical self-reflection and ongoing self-transformation in the patient. In Habermas's account, the dynamic process of psychoanalysis is fundamentally analogous to that of the Socratic dialogue, wherein reasoned self-reflection can yield enlightenment and reprieve from the constraints and impairments of false consciousness. Psychoanalysis thus conceived is a hermeneutical endeavor that allows for a decoding of the distortions that result from the activity of psychic defenses. The aim of this critical self-reflection is an action-orienting self-understanding—knowledge that passes directly and inevitably to application, insight that liberates and transfigures.

His views lead Habermas (1971) to make the controversial claim that psychoanalytic insights possess validity "only after they have been accepted as knowledge by the analysand himself"

(p. 261). By this Habermas means not that the immediate assent of the patient to a particular interpretation is a necessary condition for its truth. Resistance to interpretations is, of course, ubiquitous. Habermas is making the contextualist argument that only the overall direction and outcome of an analysis can determine the value, truth, or utility of a therapeutic construction. Analytic insights must demonstrate their validity and emancipatory efficacy in the course of therapy, for no other context is appropriate to their evaluation: "When valid, general interpretations hold . . . only to the degree that those who are made the object of individual interpretations know and recognize themselves in these interpretations. . . . *Knowledge of* the object . . . becomes *knowledge for* the object [italics mine]" (Habermas, 1971, pp. 261–262).

Ricoeur

In a manner similar to Habermas, Ricoeur (1970, 1981) contends that psychoanalysis is a form of hermeneutics. It is in his terminology a "hermeneutics of suspicion," in the tradition of those thinkers, such as Schopenhauer and Nietzsche, who viewed the manifest contents of consciousness with distrust and skepticism and believed that discovering the essence of psychic life required a probing of the latent depths of the mind. For Ricoeur, psychoanalytic concepts are analogous to the Kantian categories of understanding in that they are fundamental epistemological structures that make possible the experience of a domain of psychic and social life, one that had been obscured before the advent of psychoanalytic theory. According to Ricoeur, it is not appropriate to evaluate the tenets of psychoanalysis by the standards applied to theories in the natural sciences. Nor is the model of empirical social science appropriate to psychoanalysis. Although the findings of empirical psychology are relevant to psychoanalysis, and vice versa, the two disciplines are fundamentally different: "Psychology is an observational science dealing with the facts of behavior; psychoanalysis is an exegetical science dealing with the relationships of meaning between substitute objects and the primordial (and lost) instinctual objects. The two disciplines diverge from the very beginning, at the level of the initial notion of fact and of inference from facts" (1970, p. 359).

In the course of Ricoeur's study, psychoanalysis emerges as an interpretive discipline whose subject matter is human intentionality, or in his phrase, "the semantics of desire." Human action is seen as a text-analog, more appropriate as an object of hermeneutic inquiry than as a target for the reductionistic explanatory efforts of mainstream behavioral science. Some years earlier, the philosopher Stephen Toulmin (1954) had distinguished between causal and motivational explanations, and asserted that psychoanalytic explanations are framed in terms of the "reasons for" rather than the "causes of" behavior. Ricoeur is in partial agreement with this position, but contends that what emerges in psychoanalysis is a form of "mixed discourse" that blends cause-and-effect statements couched in the language of force and energy with motivational explanations framed in the language of intentionality. In his conception of psychoanalytic theory as a synthesis of causal explanation and the interpretation of meaning, Ricoeur (1970) suggests that psychoanalytic discourse falls outside the alternatives of motive and cause. Ricoeur, like Habermas, seems to want some distinctive status for psychoanalysis that differentiates it from the empirical sciences but also distinguishes it from other forms of hermeneutics.

Any hermeneutic reconstrual of psychoanalysis, declaring that the standards of empirical verification imported from the natural sciences are inappropriate to it, faces the inevitable question: How are psychoanalytic hypotheses to be evaluated? Ricoeur is aware of the centrality of this issue, and the importance of clarifying the epistemological foundations of psychoanalysis. We must be able, he says, to choose among competing interpretations of the same event. He writes that "an interpretation must not only be probable, but more probable than another. There are criteria of relative superiority" (1981, p. 213).

But Ricoeur also acknowledges that hermeneutic criteria of validation do not yield the certitude that attaches to the empirical sciences. Procedures of interpretive validation "are closer to a logic of probability than to a logic of empirical verification. To show that an interpretation is more probable in the light of what is known is something other than showing that a conclusion is true. In this sense, validation is not verification. Validation is an argumentative discipline comparable to the juridical procedures of legal interpretation. It is a logic of uncertainty and of qualitative probability" (1981, p. 212). Psychoanalytic interpretations are validated by argumentation among analysts who alone are cognizant of all of the tacit and manifest factors that make the psychoanalytic situation singularly meaningful and distinctive. Ricoeur (1981) goes on to offer four criteria to be used in evaluating an interpretation:

1. It is consistent with the basic tenets of psychoanalytic theory.
2. It conforms to the psychoanalytic rules for decoding the text of the unconscious.
3. It forms an intelligible narrative.
4. It is therapeutically effective when used in a therapeutic context.

Hermeneutic Psychoanalysis

Taking their inspiration and, in some cases, their formulations from Habermas and Ricoeur, several psychoanalysts have embarked on systematic critiques of the scientific pretensions of mainstream psychoanalysis. Not all of these efforts have been identified by their authors as "hermeneutic" or hermeneutically inspired. But each is informed by a common sensibility: the firm conviction that a positivistic conceptualization of the psychoanalytic treatment situation entails a misbegotten application of mechanistic concepts to a domain for which those concepts are inappropriate.

Drawing on an eclectic array of sources that includes Gadamer, Habermas, and Ricoeur, Robert Steele (1979) has boldly pronounced psychoanalysis to be not the applied empirical science its creator intended but rather a form of hermeneutics. He sees the procedures and subject matter of psychoanalysis as more akin to jurisprudence, history, and literary criticism than to engineering. Citing Dilthey's work with approval, Steele advocates the placement of psychoanalysis within the *Geisteswissenschaften,* with all the methodological and theoretical implications this would imply. He stresses the subjectivism, constructivism, and contextual specificity of the psychoanalytic situation. The aims of psychoanalysis are not those of prediction and causal analysis, but rather understanding in terms of reasons and purposes: "Psychoanalytic case histories are narratives linking the life of the individual to a general historical scheme. This scheme does not provide causes for a life, but a framework of general story elements . . . used in the reconstruction of individual life histories . . . psychoanalysis does not provide causal explanations, but reasonable interpretations that help make the past intelligible" (Steele, pp. 405–406).

For Steele the validation of psychoanalytic interpretations is to be achieved by "hermeneutic methods" brought to bear upon evidence from the psychoanalytic situation. He speaks approvingly of using the techniques and criteria from such disciplines as history, law, philosophy, and literary criticism to ascertain the adequacy of psychoanalytic explanations.

Roy Schafer, in accord with Habermas, presents a critical analysis of the mechanistic idiom of the Freudian metapsychology, which he considers to be a loose and poorly chosen set of metaphors inappropriate for explaining and rationalizing clinical realities. For Schafer the metapsychology inappropriately uses the language of forces, energies, functions, structures, apparatuses, and principles to establish and develop psychoanalysis along the lines of a physicalistic psychobiology. Schafer advocates dispensing with the metapsychology and substituting for it an "action language" of intentions, meanings, and reasons.[17]

For Schafer the move from force to action involves endorsing a philosophical position close to that of Peter Winch (1958), wherein mechanistic models and causal analysis of behavior are rejected in favor of a conception of psychoanalysis as "an essentially interpretive discipline, that is, a study of the goal-directed events that should be called actions and of the evolution of these actions in the life of the person undergoing clinical analysis" (Schafer, 1978, p. 195).

In a later work, Schafer has moved far away from Freud's metaphor of the psychoanalyst as a psychic archeologist in search of objective historical truth. Schafer (1981) has stated that psychoanalytic interpretation fundamentally involves an "act of retelling" and "narrative revision." The very facts of psychoanalysis are not the statements of the analysand. Facts are constituted and created in the systematic retelling and interpretation of the analyst. Schafer (1983) calls psychoanalysis a form of hermeneutics that seeks to create a "second reality" through its narrations. There is, for Schafer, no "final test of truth" to which the stories of psychoanalysis, the second reality, can be submitted. Seemingly wishing to place psychoanalysis within the humanities rather than the sciences, he writes: "In many ways, the second reality of psychoanalysis is more akin to the reality constructed in poetry, story, visual arts, and myth. It both supplements and competes with pragmatic conventionalized reality. Both kinds of reality are constructions. Each construction has its uses" (1983, p. 256).

Perhaps the most ambitious and extensive presentation of an alternative to the natural science model of psychoanalysis is to be found in Donald Spence's book *Narrative Truth and Historical Truth* (1982). Spence tackles head-on the problems that are central to recent debates over the epistemological status of psychoanalysis: How are we to evaluate psychoanalytic knowledge? Given the ambiguity and subjectivity of the psychoanalytic situation, can we determine the truth of the understandings reached therein? Spence's views are complex and not always logically consistent. We will discuss first his well-known view that a correspondence-based view of truth cannot be implemented in the context of psychotherapy. Central to Spence's analysis is his distinction between "historical truth" and "narrative truth."

Spence's historical truth is what we normally consider to be the aim of history: an accurate reconstruction of events as they "actually" occurred. This is the kind of truth that Freud sought in psychoanalysis and, indeed, believed to be essential to therapeutic efficacy. In his view an interpretation would be effective only if it conformed with events as they actually transpired. Freud's archeological model of psychotherapy is predicated on the search for historical truth, where truth is correspondence with some external, objective reality.

Narrative truth is a much more slippery and less intuitively clear notion. Spence has much to say about this somewhat conceptually elusive concept. Narrative truth is "the criterion we use to decide when a certain experience has been captured to our satisfaction; it depends on continuity and closure and the extent to which the fit of the pieces takes on an aesthetic finality" (1982, p. 31).

In the place of correspondence with an external reality, Spence offers aesthetic and pragmatic criteria for the evaluation of narrative truth. According to Spence, veridical reconstruction of the past is not necessary to narrative truth. Nor, contra Freud, need interpretations satisfy the criteria of historical truth to be therapeutically effective: "Interpretations are persuasive . . . not because of their evidential value but because of their rhetorical appeal; conviction emerges because the fit is good, not because we have necessarily made contact with the past" (1982, p. 32).

Spence goes a step further and reverses Freud's position on the relationship between therapeutic effectiveness and the truth of interpretations, holding that interpretations may *acquire* truth *because* they are therapeutically effective, that interpretations "become true because they serve a useful need for the patient" (1982, p. 168). To the degree that a narrative is "persuasive and compelling," Spence avers, it possesses features of narrative truth. He approvingly quotes Viderman, who contended that the analyst functions more as poet than historian. Spence likens psychoanalytic therapy to an "artistic struggle" with the patient.

Spence's concept of narrative truth incorporates several of Sherwood's criteria (1969) for the adequacy of psychoanalytic explanations, namely appropriateness, consistency, coherence, and comprehensiveness, but notably leaves out those criteria related to accuracy, that is, the degree to which psychoanalytic narratives are consistent with either empirical observations or scientifically established general truths of human behavior.

In the portion of his position described thus far, Spence (1982) is well on his way to a relativistic, constructivist account of psychoanalytic knowledge. But Spence is quite uncomfortable with some of the implications of his narrative approach. For Spence, narrative truth is problematic because of the multiplicity of interpretations that it allows. He speaks of the "embarrassing elasticity" of the psychoanalytic narrative that allows it to "embrace almost any piece of information" (p. 187). Spence regards the "flexibility" of the narrative as a serious problem, for "if narrative suitability is used to justify the truth value of a particular construction, then we begin to see that the criteria of adequacy (narrative truth) may sometimes be a poor substitute for the criteria of accuracy (historical truth) because an almost infinite number of items can be accommodated in any particular chronology" (p. 183).

Spence cannot seem to render consistent the requirements of the nomothetic explanatory science of psychoanalysis with those of the idiographic, interpretive art of psychoanalytic therapy: "What works for a particular patient at a particular time and place does not necessarily become a candidate for the general theory of psychoanalysis. . . . If we confuse narrative truth with historical (and, more generally with theoretical) truth, . . . our theory will never rise much above the level of metaphor" (1982, p. 33). Thus Spence suggests that when psychoanalysts function "as scientists" they aim to create "general laws for a general theory" and, therefore, must relinquish the "narrative tradition and adopt more conventional rules of truth finding" that involve "precise pattern match, replication, and external validation" (p. 24). They must, in essence, seek historical truth.

But for Spence narrative truth is the best we can do in the therapeutic situation. We cannot access the historical truth of the patient's life, because within the therapeutic session we cannot get back to that moment before experience was interpreted (and hence made subjective) by the analysand. Spence believes it is, in principle, possible to "get behind" the patient's words to some uninterpreted memory, some veridical copy of experience, analogous to a mental photograph. It is possible in principle, but not in practice, because of the methodological ambiguities and limitations of the psychoanalytic situation. Spence does *not* believe our inability to retrieve uninterpreted historical truth is, as some hermeneutic theorists would contend, due to the essential narrative character of human experience, that is, that there *are* no uninterpreted "brute data" of experience in the patient's life that are, in principle, recoverable if we only could gain access to them.

As Louis Sass and I (Sass & Woolfolk, 1988) pointed out, Spence's position is fundamentally inconsistent with Gadamer's view that there is no God's-eye perspective on the social world, that there are no uninterpreted "facts" behind human experience—no historical truth uninfluenced by human categories of perception and appraisal. According to Gadamer's hermeneutic view, both recollected and immediate experiences are imbued with and constituted by linguistic and cultural frameworks of meaning and significance. Interpretation is not a subsequent evaluation or transformation of raw sensory material that is made meaningful in the process of our understanding it. On the contrary, the patterning of the world is part of our original experience of it. In terms of this kind of hermeneutic position, therefore, Spence's concept of historical truth is found to be incoherent and the distinction between historical truth and narrative truth to be unsustainable. The way to make Spence's position coherent is to make it more hermeneutic. Make Spence a thoroughgoing hermeneuticist, have him understand that all events are experienced, observed, and recorded by historically situated beings who interpret at the moment of perception. Spence, perhaps cognizant of new conceptual difficulties that might follow, seems to resist such a move.

Spence is correct in his intuition that adopting a thoroughgoing hermeneutic perspective on psychotherapy may incline one toward social constructionism and epistemological relativism. Although Spence's own attempt to avoid relativism through accessing "uninterpreted" memories was unsuccessful, he was right to worry about the relativistic implications of defining truth in terms of pragmatic or aesthetic criteria. A number of writers who have followed the narrativist trail blazed by Spence and Schafer (Parry & Doan, 1994; White & Epston, 1990) are quite content to dispense with historical truth, or in some cases to dispense completely with any criterion of truth (Geha, 1993; Gergen & Kaye, 1992).

In the final chapter, I offer a critique of what I take to be some shortcomings in the various importations of hermeneutic views into psychotherapy. For now I aim to explore and describe further some of the implications of hermeneutic philosophy for our conception of psychotherapy. An important part of that endeavor is the examination of the dimensions of self-understanding, a task I take up in the next chapter.

Chapter Five

Psychotherapy and the Structure of Self-Understanding

Psychotherapies differ in the extent to which they emphasize, variously, changing oneself, knowing oneself, or enhancing one's sensitivity to experience. But whatever their emphasis, all therapies engage and influence the self-understanding of the therapy patient. Whether the paradigm involved is psychodynamic or behavioral, every session of psychotherapy involves the development and application of knowledge about the patient, much of which ultimately finds its way into the patient's self-schema.

Most of this knowledge is corrigible and impugnable. We lack secure knowledge in psychotherapy, in part, because psychology and psychiatry are at rather primitive stages of development, and we simply are ignorant of much we need to know. Some of the epistemic precariousness of psychotherapy, however, has to do with circumstances that are inevitable when what is known *generally* to be true is applied to *particular* cases, or when singular, person-specific knowledge is discovered and developed in the course of a case study.

In this chapter I attempt to say something about the kind of epistemological situation in which client and therapist are located during therapy. I also describe some hypotheses about the character of self-knowledge, emphasizing the ways in which self-understanding may be different from other forms of cognition. In so doing I aim to describe further the kind of endeavor that psychotherapy is and, inevitably, must be.

The Idiographic Nature of Psychotherapy and Self-Understanding

An important distinction that must be drawn at the outset is that between the nomothetic and the idiographic. Nomothetic knowledge is general; idiographic knowledge is specific to a particular case. Much knowledge in psychiatry and psychology is generic. Most knowledge that the therapist possesses is knowledge of generalities and is derived from theory, research, and personal experience. Psychotherapy is an application of this general knowledge to a specific case that is always, in some respects, unique. Therapeutic interventions, interpretations, and prescriptions always are directed toward an idiograph: an individual person, couple, family, or group. The therapist is always in the position of asking herself, What is going on here, with this particular case I am treating now?

In both assessment and treatment the therapist must make many decisions, such as whether to use treatment A or treatment B with a client, or whether the discontent within a marriage is due to the couple's poor conflict-resolution skills or to some more basic incompatibilities. For a client to accept a therapeutic interpretation, he must decide that it is true, not of most people but of himself. The challenge of any given case in psychotherapy is determining which generalities, to what degree, apply to that particular case. Such determinations always involve some uncertainty and may require some trial and error.

Even in applied fields derived from such systematic and unimpeachable disciplines as physics and chemistry, application to specific cases is not entirely straightforward. Mishaps occur frequently, and some practical knowledge about the particular arena of application often is required to effect a successful translation from theory to practice. Newly created airplanes may not perform aerodynamically as expected, climate control systems may not produce the temperatures intended, tunnels may collapse, winds may cause buildings to sway unacceptably, and torpedoes may bounce off the hulls of enemy ships without detonating.

Biological and psychological phenomena are more complex and variable than those of the physical sciences. They are more difficult to classify and measure. The truth about them is harder to discover and more difficult to confirm. Most research results are subject to conflicting interpretations, and debate on the clinical significance of almost any research finding often seems endless. When we do find an unchallenged truth, it commonly comes in the form of a stochastic or probabilistic generalization—for example, that smokers are twice as likely as nonsmokers to develop heart disease or that treatment A is effective 60 percent of the time whereas treatment B works 45 percent of the time. The external and ecological validities of clinical research are rarely established for the clinician. Can the treatments be implemented? Was the sample representative? Will the results generalize? These elementary questions often have no clear answers.

Now this is not to say that nomothetic research findings are without import. Often they are the very best we can do in the absence of knowledge about the particular case with which we are concerned. Most often we simply will want to play the odds, rather than function without any rational basis for choice. For example, we would be rational to use exposure methods instead of thrice-a-week psychoanalysis for the treatment of simple phobias, and to stop smoking rather than gamble that we will be among the lucky ones who escape disease. Such decisions are sensible and prudent in the absence of more certain knowledge about the case in question; for example, based on numerous unsuccessful attempts to employ tricyclic antidepressants with a particular patient, a treating psychiatrist concludes that this patient cannot tolerate the side-effects of this class of drug. But whatever the particulars may be, the logic of applying nomothetic research findings to an essentially idiographic situation such as psychotherapy requires that we recognize the uncertain and probabilistic nature of the application.

When we are confronted with an individual psychotherapy patient, even one with a clear *DSM* diagnosis, we are still ignorant about that individual and may become enlightened only after the fact, after we have tried and either succeeded or failed. Yet even after the fact clarity may not emerge. The analysis of individual cases with the aim of developing valid idiographic knowledge also is fraught with logical pitfalls, as any text on single-subject research methodology will attest. For example, a client can never know, for sure, whether it was a particular cognitive intervention that lifted his spirits or the cumulative impact of the caring and empathy provided by his therapist. Such inferences are always subject to the fallacy of *post hoc ergo propter hoc*.[18]

Each of us is, to our therapists and to ourselves, an individual case, an idiograph. Our self-knowledge is corrigible because it is prey to all the limitations of the case-study method. Self-knowledge also has additional inherent limitations and uncertainties, some of which I will describe in the sections that follow.

The Reflexivity of Self-Understanding

Self-knowledge is reflexive. It is knowledge wherein the knower is also that which is known. There is a turning of understanding back upon itself. Self is both subject *and* object.[19]

The self-reflective capacity of human beings is not something incidental to them, but rather is a fundamental, defining aspect. Kierkegaard (1849/1980, p. 13) anticipated this perspective in his characterization of the self as a "relation that relates itself to itself." We also see intimations of a reflexive conceptualization of self-knowledge in George Herbert Mead's notion (1934) of autocommunication and in Ernst Tugendhat's work (1986) on the relation of "oneself to oneself." Both Jean-Paul Sartre (1956) and Charles Taylor (1985) view self-reflection as fundamental to the ontology of persons. Sartre's formulation of being-for-itself (human being) describes it as that being which is most essentially and elementally a consciousness of consciousness, a reflection-reflecting (*reflet-reflétant*). For Taylor human selves are self-interpreting, meaning that they are, at least in part, created by their acts of self-understanding.

All these views suggest that self and self-understanding are not independent. Beliefs about the self are, in some respects, different from beliefs about other entities. If I come to alter my view of myself, this is potentially an act that is qualitatively different from a change in some other kind of belief, such as what I think to be the distance between New York and San Francisco, or whether my spouse loves me. U.S. geography is not altered by the views people have of it. My belief about my spouse may ultimately come to influence her by affecting my *behavior* toward her. But even in this instance, knower and known can be clearly separated, and any causal effect between belief and object of belief is indirect, mediated by the complexities of social interaction.

My knowledge about myself, however, affects me directly. In self-understanding, the belief and the subject matter of belief are not separable. Because my self-appraisals are fundamental to what and who I am, their metamorphoses can result in an evolution of the very person they are about. Self-understanding is in this way self-constitutive.

Self-examination is not a detached, uninfluential exploration of some invariant psychological terrain. The investigatory process itself always potentially disrupts and alters that which it studies. For example, to hear from my therapist that I "don't like myself very much" does not leave me in the position of a disinterested observer who is capable of evaluating this claim without being affected by it. The intervention of my therapist itself affects me, as does my assessment of the intervention's propositional content. As I consider the claim, reflect on it, evaluate it, these processes themselves may alter me. If I begin to think the statement to be plausible, then I may, simply on that basis, come to judge myself more or less favorably. Perhaps as it links up with my other cognitions, knowing that I have not "liked myself" provides a partial explanation and reevaluation of myself and my predicament, gives me a sense of myself as a victim of low self-esteem, and actually allows me to feel somewhat better about myself and therefore to like myself more. Conversely, for me disliking myself may signify a reprehensible form of character defect, one so distasteful that merely to have elicited the suggestion of it from a therapist is reason to shift my self-evaluation downward. But in neither case can I take seriously the interpretation's claim to truth without being affected by it in ways that may determine the interpretation's truth or falsehood.

Now the claim here is *not* that self and self-understanding are one, such that thinking something about the self makes it so. For some descriptions of ourselves to be true, our belief in them is a *necessary* but not sufficient condition. For example, I cannot be a born-again Christian without also taking on the identity, that is, believing myself to be a born-again Christian. For the most part, however, the relationship between self and self-understanding is not logical but causal, and causally quite complex.

The self-interpreting character of human beings is seen graphically in the realm of emotions and attitudes. We know that the various emotions are linked to certain patterns of cognition. Fear corresponds to an appraisal of danger; anger has its cognitive counterpart in a sense of injustice or violation. Some of the more advanced emotions, such as shame, guilt, pride, and self-hatred, not only contain an environmental appraisal but also are predicated on a conception of the self as a self-observing social actor. These emotions "involve ascribing imports that are subject-referring" and "refer us to the life of the subject *qua* subject" (Taylor, 1985, p. 59). My emotions are interlaced with my acts of cognition (as they are with my physiology and motor behavior), forming a complex structure of inextricably intertwined, reciprocally interacting features of my response to the world. Much of what we know is not known dispassionately, but is the very ground of our emotional life.

Examining our emotions, understanding them and their bases more fully, may lead to their alteration. Years of rage may dissipate when I learn that a perceived betrayal was inadvertent or motivated by some noble purpose. An insight into my self or my circumstances may lead me to decide that amorous feelings are infatuation rather than durable and transcendent love and, in so doing, change what it *is*, in fact, that I do feel: "Why should it be that coming to see (or feel) that certain terms properly describe our emotions often involves shaping (reshaping) those emotions? This is because our subject-referring feelings are given their character by the sense of the import they incorporate; when this sense alters in an important way, then the feeling changes. But because of the problematic nature of our self-understanding, a number of different accounts are possible; and these, by changing our understanding of the import, also change the emotions we can experience" (Taylor, 1985, p. 70).

In some cases developing self-understanding is a matter of analyzing, defining, and articulating the attributes that potentially *could* describe us, while concurrently, in parallel fashion, assessing whether these attributes *do* describe us. Many people who enter psychotherapy label themselves "unhappy" and are seeking happiness through therapy. Many find it. But the process is not exclusively that of changing one's life so as to find the new life satisfactory in terms of those criteria one originally brought into therapy. This kind of change frequently does occur, but it is also often the case that one's definition of "happiness" and one's criteria for a satisfactory life are altered over the course of therapy. So when we seek to explore the applicability of certain labels or descriptions to ourselves, we may change our understanding, our very definitions, of those labels. A young man who believes that the essence of courage lies in aggressive, violent action may, in the exploration of his own courage over time and in various situations, come to reshape his concept of valor to include acts of peaceful civil disobedience, such as those of Gandhi or King, and in the process come to rate his own courage differently in light of his altered view. Loving relationships, if they are lengthy, may occasion many reevaluations of the strength and depth of the caring bond. But it is not just one's lover and the nature of the relationship that are explored, revised, and better understood over time. It is also the meaning and significance of the terms *love, commitment,* and *caring* that come to be amended.

When we inquire into ourselves, the tools of our inquiry can modify and transform the object under investigation. There is a certain type of indeterminacy in self-understanding, a plasticity in selfhood that results from the reflexive epistemology of self-understanding. Any time one gets an interpretive fix on one's own self, there is the potential that the self will not remain as it was before.

The Self as Narrative and Historical

As Ulric Neisser (1988) has told us, the self is, in part, created by memory. I come to know who I am by recollecting a past, by experiencing the unity and continuity of my personhood across time and circumstance. This personal past belonging to each of us is not experienced as a disconnected jumble of scenes and mental snapshots. It possesses what literary theorists call "narrative flow," a kind of coherence of theme that serves both to frame the relationships among the episodes of one's life and also to characterize the overall direction and significance of that life. One's present self becomes intelligible within the context of a remembered past and an anticipated future that are conceived as components of a unity. The sense of self is that of a protagonist in a story or a collection of stories.

A number of writers (Carr, 1986; Crites, 1971; Polkinghorne, 1988) would contend that narrative is a fundamental structure of self-understanding, one that is necessary to the very existence of the self. Self-understanding and, therefore, the self are rooted in narrative. It is only in constructing our stories, which we tell to others and to ourselves, that we achieve personhood. It is only when we have interpreted and understood ourselves and our worlds and have woven this understanding into stories that we become fully human. To be a self means to exist as a purposive entity embedded within webs of meaning, and as a continuity across time, one that is articulated through narrative: "People use self-stories to interpret and account for their lives. The basic dimension of human existence is temporality, and narrative transforms the mere passing away of time into a meaningful unity, the self. The study of a person's own experience of her or his life-span requires attending to the operations of the narrative form and to how this life story is related to the stories of others" (Polkinghorne, 1988, p. 119).

The construction of narratives would seem to be a fundamental human proclivity. Roland Barthes (1977) has observed that narrative has an almost infinite number of forms, including myth, fable, painting, drama, cinema, journalism, and conversation. Frederick Jameson (1981, p. 13) describes narrative as the "central function or *instance* of the human mind." Lewis Mink (1981, p. 239) refers to narrative as a "primary and irreducible" mode of human comprehension. Arthur Danto (1985) argues that narration is one of our basic modes of representing the world. We are predisposed to perceive the world in the language of "beginnings and endings, and turning points and crises and climaxes" (p. xiii). In several empirical studies of object perception where the movements of multiple geometric figures served as stimuli, observers were inclined to create stories in which human-like motives were attributed to the abstract shapes (Heider & Simmel, 1944; Michotte, 1946/1963). Alasdair MacIntyre argues not only that narrative is often the framework of choice in explaining the social world but also that human activity has an *inherent* narrative quality: "Human life has a determinate form, the form of a certain kind of story. It is not just that poems and sagas narrate what happens to men and women, but that in their narrative form poems and sagas capture a form that was already present in the lives which they relate" (MacIntyre, 1981, p. 117).

Narrative is a buzzword in the humanities and social sciences today. Some see it as a link between the sciences and humanities, the common explanatory form that may unite differing traditions of explanation and understanding. Personality psychologists suggest that identity development over the life span is felicitously conceived as the continuous authoring of one's personal narrative (McAdams, 1996). Some psychotherapists have become so captivated by the concept of narrative that they believe that understanding and "rewriting" personal narratives is the fundamental process in psychotherapy (Omer & Strenger, 1992; White & Epston, 1990).

When psychotherapy patients are helped to understand their lives, narrative forms undoubtedly play a great role. This is seen clearly in Freudian psychoanalysis, wherein identifying the "correct" story is, in some sense, the essence of the treatment. It could be argued that settling on a "salutary" story is an essential aspect of therapy even when the therapy does not emphasize the construction or reconstruction of personal histories. Part of the function of any therapy is to provide a coherent explanation of why the client has problems, to generate a "story" that allows the client to make sense out of his difficulties. This is the case even in those present-centered therapies (such as cognitive-behavior therapy) that regard extensive knowledge of one's personal history to be unimportant in ameliorating problems of living. The narratives of such therapies are not comprehensive accounts of an individual's psychic development but rather are more specific stories of the genesis and maintenance of particular patterns of affect and behavior.

The Historicity of Narrative

To some extent, narrative is history. There are limits on the objectivity that can be achieved by history. To the extent that the interpretations and inferences drawn during the course of psychotherapy involve history, they too are subject to an inherent uncertainty.

Kierkegaard (1843/1959) once wrote that we live our lives forward but we understand them backward. At any given time, the future is unknown to us. We cannot state with any degree of certainty how the present moment will appear from the perspective of the future. We can attempt to predict future occurrences, as science often does, but we have no knowledge of the future to employ in our descriptions of present events. Describing the past is different in this regard. We know some of the future of the past, that which extends from a past event to the present moment. Our narrative-historical descriptions of past events are framed in relation to events that occurred afterward. Danto (1985, p. xii) tells us that narration involves giving "descriptions of events under which the events could not have been witnessed, since they make essential reference to events later in time than the events they are about." Unlike history, science is a creature of the present. The descriptions of events in science do not require future developments to contextualize them.

Danto (1985) illustrates the distinctive endeavor that is narrative-historical explanation by positing an "Ideal Chronicler," an omniscient entity who knows "whatever happens at the moment it happens" (p. 149). The Ideal Chronicler, furthermore, has the capacity of instantaneous transcription so that all events are recorded at the moment of their occurrence. But despite possessing what would seem to be all the requisites necessary for the writing of an "objective" historical account, the Ideal Chronicler is fundamentally inadequate to the task. This is because the "truth concerning an event can only be known after, and sometimes only *long* after the event itself has taken place, and this part of the story historians alone can tell. It is something even the best sort of witness cannot know" (p. 151).

For example, the Ideal Chronicler could observe the outbreak of war in Europe in 1618. But what we now know to be the true description of that war, the "Thirty Years War," cannot be applied to this conflagration any earlier than 1648. Nor could we speak in 270 B.C. of the heliocentric theory of Aristarchus of Samos "anticipating" the work of Copernicus, nor of the ultimate role that the cotton economy of the antebellum South would play in the evolution of the U.S. political system. As Danto puts it, to describe an event completely "is to locate it in all the right stories," which we cannot do for contemporary events because we are "temporally provincial with regard to the future" (1985, p. 142). The effects, implications, and ramifications of events that are part of a "complete" historical account of them can be known only in the light of a future to which they give rise. And this future is open and unknown.

In a similar fashion, self-understanding and, therefore, the self are contingent and indeterminate because of the uncertainty of the future. Sartre argues that human being, being-for-itself, is distinguished by its plasticity, incompleteness, and openness to the future. It is death only that finishes the story of a life. My self-narrative is under continual revision as I look backward and reinterpret it in the light of my present, and reorder, relabel, and reevaluate the data of my past. Because we do not know what that future will be and what reinterpretations of self it will occasion, the self remains indefinite. Self and future are involved in a loop of mutual influence: self-interpretation is revised by the future, but the future also is influenced by the generative and creative by-products of self-interpretation. My self-understanding is one factor that produces my future.

Narrative Structure

Narratives have configural properties, such that the whole of a narrative is greater than the sum of its parts. A simple ordering of events in time produces what historians call a chronicle, but not a narrative. The components of a narrative are understood in relation to some theme that both organizes and interrelates its parts and explains their meaning and significance. Over and above the temporal organization of the chronicle, narratives have "plots." Plots are not only frameworks within which complicated part-whole relationships are elucidated, but are also themselves gestalts possessing direction and cogency. Narratives have force and import; they make some kind of point.

Both the historical properties of narratives, described in the previous section, and their formal properties indicate a role for hermeneutic methods in their assessment and evaluation. The part-whole relation that describes the operation of the hermeneutic circle is present in narrative. Part cannot be understood except in relation to whole, and comprehending the whole derives from an understanding of parts and their interrelation. The goals of objectivity and value-neutrality seem less plausible for the analysis of narrative than, say, for the understanding of molecular thermodynamics. The component events of a narrative find their way into the story only after having been "selected" and "described" on the basis of acts of interpretation that are grounded in human interests. Even if one believes the currently fashionable "postempiricist" view that there are hermeneutic dimensions in all scientific explanation, including the physical sciences (Kuhn, 1970; Hesse, 1980), clearly much scientific data lacks the degree of preinterpretation possessed by the human situations captured in narratives.

Narratives also possess aesthetic, moral, and rhetorical properties that we usually do not associate with the stereotype of objective science. There is an expressive richness to the narrative that is missing from more sterile acts of cognition. Events are brought to life and given complex resonances when they are woven into a story. Clearly part of the appeal of narrative is to faculties other than the intellect. Narratives frequently, perhaps inevitably (White, 1973) serve to affect, to judge, to persuade. They are speech acts and forms of discourse with functions broader and more complex than those of scientific explanation.

To summarize this section, if we are partially constituted by our self-narratives, we are historical, moral, and aesthetic works in progress. The comprehension of the narrative aspects of selfhood will likely require analytical tools that are not commonly associated with the sciences, but rather with the interpretive traditions of the humanities. Comprehensive self-understanding will require interpretive methods and thus entail a hermeneutic of selfhood.

Self-Understanding as Personal Metaphysics

There are two more dimensions of self-understanding that reveal just what a hazy and problematic entity it is. One important aspect of self-knowledge involves the assessment of which aspects of our bodies, our minds, and our behavior lie within the reach of our volition. In coming to know ourselves, we delineate the limits of our causal powers, establishing wherein we are free and wherein we are determined. The second important component of our

understanding of self has to do with self-evaluation: locating ourselves and our actions in relation to our standards of virtue and peccability and with respect to our tastes and preferences. Both these
activities are inevitable aspects of self-appraisal and both are
orchestrated within conceptual frameworks wherein "objective"
knowledge is difficult to come by. Such pursuits are more akin to
developing a personal philosophical anthropology than they are to
conducting a scientific assessment of the self.

Our Causal Powers

We experience ourselves sometimes as making choices and carry-
ing them out, but at other times as feeling that some reaction of
ours results from factors beyond our control. This distinction
between the voluntary and involuntary is fundamental to our ordinary, everyday discourse, to our common sense, and to our folk psychology. The distinction between freedom and necessity is central
to our social cognition and to most of our cultural practices—for
example, law, ethics, and education. Our self-knowledge is to some
extent the story of how these two domains of freedom and necessity fit together in our lives. Establishing the limits of our freedom
is a dilemma for each of us.

This partitioning of our worlds, into those domains where we
have freedom of choice and those where we do not, occurs in every
form of psychotherapy. A psychoanalyst may view my emotional
response to a coworker as a transference-like reaction inexorably
dictated by dramas enacted in early childhood, whereas an existential therapist may see such feelings as the result of decisions
freely made. In therapy I may learn to forgive myself, give myself a
break, and stop being so hard on myself by accepting that I am not
responsible for many of the events that occur in my life. But I may
just as likely learn to stop complaining, making excuses, and blam-
ing external circumstances, as I begin to take responsibility for the
reactions I experience and the behavior I display. Every form of
therapy encompasses what Ricoeur calls mixed discourse, a blend

of the language of autonomy and intention with the idiom of necessity and cause. And every approach to psychotherapy takes a metatheoretical stand on the relative proportions of our lives that are or can be brought under our control, what we can and cannot alter. Indeed, one of the social functions of psychotherapy is to produce explanatory frameworks that give us answers to questions regarding the extent and limits of our malleability and, therefore, our freedom and responsibility. Therapy tells us when to struggle, when to exert the will, and when to relent and go with the flow of implacable fortune and proclivity.

Scientists and humanists agree that there are limits on freedom of the will. The role of necessity in human existence and its constraints on the individual will are acknowledged in every worldview, whether primitive or modern. Even that extreme proponent of human freedom, Jean-Paul Sartre, recognized that a waiter could not choose to be a minister of France. For contemporary people it is not the gods but nature that restricts our choices. We look to science for a mapping of nature and for a spelling out of human capacities. Science has uncovered some limits on human volition, and undoubtedly will uncover more. In this vein, using the latest research data, Martin Seligman (1994) has produced an admirable analysis of the plasticity of human beings and of what the existentialists would call our "unfreedom."

Of course, for reasons stated earlier, scientific studies cannot provide each individual human being with a complete account of what she can and cannot choose to do. The stochastic nature of biological and psychological research data make their application to specific individual cases problematic. For example, I can never know with certainty whether, with some greater exertion of the will, I could have passed up that cigarette or gotten along better with my in-laws.

The bases on which people are held responsible for their acts within a society tell us much about that society's image of humanity. From our present enlightened scientific vantage point some past parsings of freedom and necessity seem rather foolish and peremptory. But no matter what scientific advances the future brings, some behavior will likely always be describable in the ordinary vernacular of choice and intention, even if an alternative description in a more deterministic idiom also is available. For example, even if it is the case that John became a political radical because of his birth order or his genes, it is also the case that he came to see the current power structure as corrupt and effete, and chose to embrace radical politics. Scientists doing science will probably not use behavioral science jargon to describe their own scientific activities, certainly not those they wish to take credit for.[20] They probably will see themselves as inventing theories, formulating and testing hypotheses, and choosing among available explanations of the data.

The Evaluative Topography of the Self

In Chapter Two I described how the value-laden nature of psychotherapy derives to some degree from its social functions as a proto-ethics and an instrument of social control. To the extent that psychotherapy plays those roles it will necessarily contain evaluative elements. But the normative character of psychotherapy derives also from the essentially value-laden nature of self-appraisal and social cognition.

A number of psychologists and philosophers have taken the position that values are central features of selfhood. Developmental psychologists have suggested that the emergence of a system of values is a critical feature of identity development (Erikson, 1968; Kegan, 1982). Several philosophers (Frankfurt, 1971; Taylor, 1988; Tugendhat, 1986) have contended that some of what it means to be a person or human agent is to have values and to be able and inclined to reflect upon those values. Taylor (1988, p. 298) writes: "Being a self is existing in a space of issues, [having] to do with how one ought to be, or how one measures up against what is good, what is right, and what is really worth doing. It is being able to find one's standpoint in this space, being able to occupy, to be a perspective in it."

Harry Frankfurt (1971) has described a feature unique to human self-understanding, the formation and analysis of "second-order" evaluations, evaluations of the norms that guide our first-order evaluations. This operation is a kind of reflective self-appraisal or metacognition. Second-order evaluation is our own reflection upon and assessment of the values we consciously hold or that are implied by our actions. Thus we may covet money but wish that we did not. Conversely, we may take pride in the generosity we display in making donations to charitable causes. Much of our sense of self-respect has to do with whether we live up to our expectations of ourselves (our values). Self-esteem also derives from second-order evaluations, from how estimable or base we deem our desires and motives to be.

Empirical research has indicated that human social cognition is organized around value (Gara & Rosenberg, 1979; Kim & Rosenberg, 1980; Woolfolk, Novalany, Gara, Allen, & Polino, 1995; Zajonc, 1980). Our perceptions and cognitions of ourselves and of other people, no matter how heterogeneous they appear to be, tend to cohere on a single dimension that is most aptly conceptualized as evaluation (that is, good-bad, positive-negative). The greatest amount of semantic information conveyed by any label applied to the self (whether it has to do with intelligence, beauty, or personality) is the degree to which it is regarded as desirable or undesirable, admirable or unadmirable. Evaluation is the principal axis of self-appraisal.

Self-appraisal, consequently, occurs in relation to standards of worth. These standards are not reducible to any objectivistic, value-free categorical scheme. Self-understanding therefore entails making value-judgments about oneself. Validating or invalidating such judgments, in or out of the therapeutic context, inevitably will take a form closer to philosophical discussion than to scientific testing.[21]

To summarize, self-understanding is fundamentally about determining one's capacities and one's worth. But these are not topics that can be exhausted by appeals to "objective" evidence or to some evaluatively neutral body of empirical research. These matters inevitably involve judgments of value and the taking of some philosophical position with respect to freedom and determinism. Thus to the extent that psychotherapy directly addresses self-understanding, and thereby the issues of worth and freedom, it deviates from a technological mode into a form that is philosophical and normative.

Practical Self-Understanding

Some of our acts of self-understanding have to do with matters that concern us little. For example, I personally can ponder dispassionately and disinterestedly whether I am a good backgammon player or whether my height is 6 feet 2¼ inches or 6 feet 2½ inches. But much self-understanding is of a different kind. Much of it involves cognition on which practical, everyday activity is predicated. This area of self-understanding has consequential implications for our happiness and well-being. Knowledge about whether I am able to do my job, meet the expectations of a friend, or truly enjoy a performance of La Traviata to which I have been invited has a different status. It is a cognitive map we use to navigate the terrain of everyday life. This kind of understanding is what we employ in deciding "what to do" in the course of mundane, daily existence. In Habermas's vernacular, this kind of self-understanding is action-orienting. It guides us in the selection of careers and spouses, in the allocation of time and resources, in our assessments of self and others. This kind of practical self-understanding is central to what is sought and found in psychotherapy. I turn to this topic in the next chapter.

Chapter Six

Psychotherapy and Practical Knowledge

In the final section of the preceding chapter I argued that a practical dimension is inherent to self-understanding. I further suggested that the practical aspects of self-understanding are not readily subsumed within an "objective" scientific account. Before fully drawing out the implications of these contentions for psychotherapy, I should like to clarify what I mean by the term *practical*. Practice is often defined by contrasting it with theory or with research. We are all familiar with the many different polarities that have been used to characterize the differences between practice and its counterpoints: common sense–book learning; implementation–policy; applied–basic; real world–ivory tower; practical–theoretical. In the mental health professions we have our versions of this opposition: clinic versus laboratory and clinical practice versus academic research.

The upshot of this meditation on the practical is the suggestion that psychotherapy is a practical endeavor aimed at the practical aspects of patients' lives. Because it is applied in the real world to problems of living occurring within the unique, complex, and variable life contexts of self-interpreting beings, psychotherapy can never derive from behavioral science to the extent that mechanical engineering derives from physics. Psychotherapy will always involve wisdom as well as expertise, pedagogy as well as technology. This humanistic residuum remains in psychotherapy *not* because we are unable, in principle, to transform certain technical aspects of psychotherapy into a set of standardized, rigorously evaluated treatment manuals. We can do this and should do this, to some degree. What we cannot do is make our lives or the lives of our patients into material that can be encompassed completely by science and technique.

Everydayness

The practical sphere is often identified with the concept of the *life-world* that comes to us from Husserl. Heidegger used the term *everydayness* more or less synonymously. The lifeworld simply refers to the realm of ordinary, common-sense experience. Each of us takes his or her own lifeworld "for granted," adopting a "natural attitude" of "naive realism" (Heider, 1958) that is prescientific and pretheoretical. In the lifeworld the pragmatic motive predominates (Schutz, 1962). There, each of us is attuned to what "works" for us in attaining those smaller and larger objectives that are the focus of our daily activities. Self-knowledge derived from everyday life experience is framed most often within the boundaries of our personal concerns and our efforts to orchestrate our lives around those concerns.

Science is an outgrowth of everydayness and is predicated on it. As Bubner (1981, p. 130) has put it: "scientific knowledge finds its place in a broadly conceived context of '*pre-understanding*.' The pre-understanding of activity in the life-world, prior to methodically regulated scientific operations, actually makes enquiry possible. . . . The conditions for the possibility of scientific activity lie in an original familiarity with reality, in skilled practical dealings with things and implements, in the ability to acquire techniques and to master special procedures and not least in the interest in problems which require solution." Science never replaces the lifeworld completely for any of us. It simply provides alternative descriptions and explanations of components of the ordinary reality we take for granted. No matter what our level of scientific sophistication, for practical purposes we still consider tables to be solid objects rather than combinations of empty space and microscopic entities (molecules and the like) too small to see. In the practical sphere, a telephone is a tool for talking; a computer is a box that accepts and represents keystrokes; our bodies are forms to be clothed; and so on. Sometimes, for certain endeavors, we may value science over the natural attitude. Indeed, in certain highly technical domains, such as electrical engineering, virtually all the acumen involved may be science-derived and abstracted from ordinary everydayness.

Everyday cognition and problem solving are similar to scientific thinking in many obvious ways, as George Kelly (1955) was fond of pointing out. Yet there are important disanalogies between the world of scientific inquiry and that of everyday coping. The scientist strives (albeit sometimes unsuccessfully) to be disinterested, incredulous, and intellectually meticulous. Yet in our everyday lives such goals are often neither realizable nor appropriate. We are too much concerned with the outcomes of our actions to function dispassionately. To function effectively we frequently must suspend our disbelief and skepticism. Frequently we must be prepared to act on data and inferences that would not meet the standards applied to scientific research. In everyday life, information is corrigible, and there are too many issues requiring action and too little time to study each and every one adequately. Because of our engagement in our own lives and the practical exigencies we must confront, we do not, cannot, live our everyday lives as scientists.

Science cannot supersede the lifeworld completely for other reasons as well. Two aspects of the lifeworld that science cannot entirely assimilate are (1) the background of tacit assumptions and practices on which science, and all abstract knowledge, is predicated and (2) the sociohistorical context of human interests that both shape science and ultimately determine its application.

The Background and Tacit Knowledge

The Background is a matrix of tacit assumptions about physical and social reality that is the foundation of all our activities in the world. It has been described, variously, by Ludwig Wittgenstein, Martin Heidegger, John Searle, Pierre Bourdieu, and Hubert Dreyfus. The

Background contains the taken-for-granted knowledge and norms that are implicit in both our mundane and theoretical activities. The Background is pervasive, and so complex that it can never be made entirely explicit.

Searle (1995) argues that the Background, meaning a practical assumptive context, is necessary for determining the truth of any assertion. According to Searle, the literal meaning of a sentence is not sufficient for determining its truth or falsehood. To ascertain truth, in addition to literal meaning we require a "Background of capacities, dispositions, know-how, etc., which are not themselves part of the semantic content of the sentence" (p. 130). For example, in the sentences "Susie cut the cake" or "Susie cut the grass" the verb "to cut" has a constant literal meaning. There is no metaphor involved, as in the sentence "Susie cut class." But even in the first two cases, where literal meaning is constant, what counts as "cutting" is a function of its linguistic context. If Susie approaches the cake with a lawn mower or the grass with a knife, we would feel something to be amiss and that neither aforementioned sentence correctly describes the action. But this failure of the descriptions to satisfy truth conditions in these odd cases has nothing to do with the literal meaning of the sentences. The descriptions fail because our understanding the verb differently in different situations depends on a context of cultural practices (the Background), and this context is an implicit part of the descriptions. Learning to use the Background to interpret meaning is analogous to learning decorum—for example, learning how far to stand from another person while conversing so as not to invade that person's "space." Features of the Background can be made explicit, but typically are not.

The anthropologist Bourdieu (1990) has proposed a version of the Background that he calls *habitus*. The habitus can be thought of as a kind of cultural preconscious, a repository of "durable, transposable dispositions, structured structures predisposed to function as . . . principles which generate and organize practices and representations that can be objectively adapted to their outcomes without presupposing a conscious aiming at ends or an express mastery of the operations necessary in order to attain them" (p. 53). The habitus contains the habits and skills that are necessary to function in any society. The know-how of the habitus is acquired by members of a society in the various ways that human beings learn: observation and imitation, conditioning, and explicit instruction. The habitus is the source of common sense and social custom. But, for the most part, it remains tacit. Specifying all the features of the habitus would be an infinite and futile task. Even small domains of the habitus cannot be entirely comprehended by explicit propositions or rules.

William James (1878/1978) gave us the distinction between *knowledge-by-acquaintance* and *knowledge-about*. This distinction corresponds, roughly, to the difference in meaning between *noscere*, *kennen*, and *connaître*, on the one hand, and *scire*, *wissen*, and *savoir*, on the other. I can know Paris, in the sense that I know my way around Paris and am experienced in dealing with the city. Knowledge-by-acquaintance requires direct experience, that is, spending time in Paris. It is not always easily or completely articulable, comprising impressions, habits, images, dispositions, and feelings. I can also know *about* Paris without ever having been there or without having any particular skill in dealing with the city. I can know many definite facts about Paris, its population, the distance from Sainte-Chapelle to the Musée Marmottan, and so on. Knowledge-about is definite, specific, and propositional in form. Its apprehension is not contingent on experience within in a particular situation.

Concepts analogous to knowledge-by-acquaintance and the Background figure in the philosophy of science. Polanyi's concept (1958) of tacit knowledge would seem to be closely related to James's view of knowledge-by-acquaintance. The know-how required to be a scientist is a complex set of skills, practical knowledge, and predilections, most of which are tacit and which Polanyi asserts can be acquired only through apprenticeship. Scientific activity rests on an unarticulated foundation of implicit assumptions, shared understandings, and agreed-upon procedures that make up what Thomas Kuhn (1970) calls the "disciplinary matrix" of a science. This tacit background of scientific practice cannot be fully explicated; rather it is acquired by scientists during their training through such activities as working through problems and conducting experiments that are exemplary for a particular scientific field. Scientific *theory* abstracts phenomena from their contexts of human relevance and enunciates explanations of causal relations among them, that is, scientific *knowledge*. But scientific *practice* itself cannot be made entirely explicit or reduced to any formulaic set of guidelines.

In several empirical studies of what they term "practical intelligence," Sternberg, Wagner and their colleagues (Sternberg, Wagner, Williams, & Horvath, 1995; Wagner & Sternberg, 1986) have suggested that all fields incorporate knowledge that is practical versus academic, informal versus formal, and usually not taught overtly. These investigators find that scientists who are universally recognized as "expert" and "successful" have a kind of informal know-how that is implicit. Some of this practical knowledge can be made explicit, but much of it is "disorganized and relatively inaccessible, making it potentially ill suited for direct instruction" (Wagner & Sternberg, p. 54).

In sources as diverse as Heideggerian philosophy, Wittgenstein's writings, and the ideas of the American Pragmatists, there is a claim that some forms of knowing involve skill or know-how, as opposed to explicit propositional knowledge. For Heidegger, the most basic kind of understanding is exemplified in our everyday skillful coping with the environment through the use of tools and equipment (Dreyfus, 1991). For example, the most primordial understanding of "hammers" and "hammering," to use Heidegger's favorite illustration, does not involve representational knowledge of the shapes and sizes of hammers and the various uses to which they are put. Knowing hammers, in this sense, means knowing how to use them, knowing how to hammer. Wittgenstein (1953) also

asserted a close relationship between linguistic meaning and linguistic use, between understanding and behavior. For Wittgenstein,
understanding a rule is most essentially not a matter of cognitive
representation but rather of being able to follow the rule, of being
able to participate satisfactorily in the social practices governed by
the rule. Dewey (1922, p. 177) also sees unarticulated skills and
habits as forms of knowledge: "We walk and read aloud, we get off
and on streetcars, we dress and undress, and perform a thousand
useful acts without thinking of them. We know something, namely,
how to do them."

No doubt psychotherapists have tacit knowledge. In this they
are not professionally unique. Undoubtedly diamond cutters,
painters, and streetcar conductors do, too. Certainly phrenologists
and alchemists also possessed their own stores of tacit knowledge.
Some of the tacit knowledge involved in being a therapist, however, is likely different from that of the plumber or the mathemati-
cian. The entire subject matter of psychotherapy is the lives of
patients, which are themselves contextualized within a background
of tacit knowledge. The tacit knowledge of the therapist is often of
a second order, that is, tacit knowledge about tacit knowledge. The
therapist must not only absorb the tacit knowledge of the psychotherapy profession but also be knowledgeable in the ways of the
cultural Background and the problems and opportunities it can create for clients. Ideally a therapist should be knowledgeable both in
the craft of therapy and in the ways of the world.

In most psychotherapy, therapists and clients share a common
cultural Background. Conducting therapy with a patient from a different culture is challenging because therapists have difficulty comprehending and giving the right meaning to the material that a
culturally dissimilar client presents (Sue & Sue, 1990). Misunder-
standings of various kinds are common. The idiom of psychotherapy in such cases may require arduous and meticulous translations
as client and therapist struggle to find a common ground of meanings and values.

Engagement and Evaluation

Over a hundred years ago William James proclaimed that human beings bring their concerns, purposes, and values to all acts of knowing. We bring to cognition "interests" that are the "very flour out of which our mental dough is kneaded" (James, 1878/1978, p. 21). We human selves are not mere spectators at the game of life; we are *players*; we are *in* the game. Heidegger expressed a similar view in his discussion of "affectedness" (*Befindlichkeit*). In his philosophy, one of the most general characteristics of human being (*Dasein*) is that things *matter* to us. We live our lives not as disinterested observers of events but rather as engaged participants whose existences are consequential to us. Two aspects of our engaged relationship with the world are values and emotions.

Conventional conceptions of psychotherapy hold that the client's emotions are a principal focus of psychotherapy but that the client's value system should not be tampered with. Influencing the client's values, it is thought, would constitute a departure from objective and disinterested professional practice. Yet any relatively rudimentary understanding of the topography of emotion convinces us that values and emotions are inseparable. Emotions fundamentally are evaluative responses.[22] Certain emotions are so inextricably intertwined with moral judgments that they cannot be addressed in any practical endeavor without also encompassing the values connected with them.

The relationship between values and emotions is essential. The philosopher Robert Kane (1994) identifies the "positive" emotions (such as joy) with what he terms *basic value experiences* and the "negative" emotions (such as sadness) with what he labels *basic disvalue experiences*. The view here, which originated with Spinoza, is that emotions are the elemental prototypic experiences whereby "we come to distinguish and define good and evil in the first place. Such experiences are like windows through which value first enters into our human world" (Kane, p. 52).

The more complex self- or other-referring emotions, discussed in the previous chapter, are straightforwardly moral and evaluative, as an exploration of their experiential features reveals. Guilt is perhaps the most obviously moral emotion, felt when we believe ourselves to have committed, or we wish to commit, an act we find wrongful (Lazarus, 1991). Shame is a close relative of guilt, involving global self-devaluation and feelings of disgrace following our failure to live up to a standard held to be important by ourselves or others (Lewis, 1993). The moral component of anger was described by Aristotle (trans. 1991, p. 142), who defined it as follows: "Desire, accompanied by pain, for revenge for an obvious belittlement of oneself or of one's dependents, the belittlement being *uncalled for* [italics mine]."[23] This view of anger as the emotion elicited by the actions of other people, actions perceived to be illegitimate or unethical, continues to form the basis for contemporary concepts of anger (Rozin, Haidt, & McCauley, 1993; Sabini & Silver, 1982). Disgust and contempt are evaluative emotions related to anger, but commonly are educed by events outside the moral realm, for example, events that produce negative aesthetic evaluations.

The preceding analysis of emotion implies that any undertaking, such as psychotherapy, that describes, analyzes, discovers, or modifies emotion will be deeply involved in moral-evaluative material. When one engages a person's pattern of emotional responses to the world, one engages her value system as well. With his characteristic perspicacity, Albert Ellis (1962, 1973) realized this many years ago. For Ellis, psychotherapy is in part an attempt to convert the patient from an unhealthy, irrational set of values to a system of values that is rational and, therefore, salubrious.

Clearly one of the functions of psychotherapy is to help us come to grips with the realm of our values and emotions. Therapy aims to help us discover, understand, clarify, unpack, manage, control, and modify our feelings and attitudes. Much of the evaluative and emotional know-how sought and often achieved in psychotherapy is explicit and is articulated over the course of therapy.

Getting "in touch" with one's emotional life requires not only sensitivity to affective experience but also learning to label feelings explicitly and to make discriminations among them.

In his theory of multiple intelligences, Howard Gardner (1983) discusses some aspects of the kind of understanding that pertains to values and emotions. He contends that the manifold capacities possessed by human beings can be placed into a category scheme that describes our diverse talents. He sets forth the standard classes of intellectual aptitude (for example, spatial relations ability) but also delineates a category that comprises emotional and social know-how. Gardner dubs this kind of ability the "personal intelligences." Personal intelligence comes in two varieties. Intrapersonal intelligence is directed toward practical self-understanding and self-knowledge. Gardner stresses, as central to this ability, self-awareness and, especially, awareness of one's emotions. High intrapersonal intelligence involves the ability to make discriminations among one's feelings and "to label them, to enmesh them in symbolic codes, to draw upon them as a means of understanding and guiding one's behavior" (Gardner, p. 239). The second variety, interpersonal intelligence, is simply "people skills": the ability to "size up" other people, to identify and distinguish among their various moods, motivations, temperaments, and proclivities. Gardner suggests that the personal intelligences may be culturally situated to the extent that know-how essential to effective functioning in a given culture can be grasped by someone from an alien culture only with great difficulty. This observation also suggests that the personal intelligences involve some ability to comprehend the cultural Background.

In related work, Salovey and Mayer (1990) have described a construct they label *emotional intelligence*. Emotional intelligence turns out to be an aggregation of Gardner's two forms of personal intelligence. Salovey and Mayer describe five domains of emotional intelligence:

1. Awareness and knowledge of one's emotions

2. Managing one's emotions

3. Motivating oneself

4. Identifying other people's emotions

5. Managing one's interpersonal relationships

Daniel Goleman's recent book (1995) reviews much of the empirical research on emotional intelligence and argues convincingly that emotional intelligence helps us achieve physical health, succeed in our careers, and prosper within our families. Recent work in evolutionary psychology (Buss, 1991; Tooby & Cosmides, 1990) indicates that emotional intelligence has always been important, both to the viability of the species and to the success of individual members.

The work of Sternberg and Wagner and their colleagues on practical intelligence (cited earlier) converges with the work on emotional intelligence. These investigators have determined that the self-knowledge one has about one's "own individual motives and goals" is a critical aspect of practical intelligence that facilitates success in a wide array of fields. London (1995) has reviewed research indicating that accurate self-appraisal is an aid to career success and to effective functioning within organizations. Understanding one's strengths and weaknesses, as well as knowing what one really wants, can be helpful in guiding the use of talents and proclivities.

Effectiveness in life is something we instantly recognize in others. We know it when we see it because of the results it brings, yet the qualities possessed by effective people can be difficult to specify or to teach. "Style," "sensitivity," "charm," "self-awareness," and "charisma" cannot be produced by a packaged treatment manual or a set of explicit, standardized instructions. Such formulaic attempts degenerate into parody and are the stuff of late-night television comedy.

Practical know-how in the realm of relationships and emotions is among the most important and valuable things a person can possess. There are theories explaining this know-how, and it has been studied empirically. It is also sought and found with great regularity in psychotherapy. It is, in some respects, the basic stuff of psychotherapy—emotions and relationships. The concept of emotional intelligence enables us to achieve yet another perspective on psychotherapy, as neither essentially technology nor art, but as a form of education: the pedagogy of emotional intelligence.

There are obviously many schools of thought on how to deal with one's emotions. The various approaches to psychotherapy could be distinguished on the basis of their positions on the role of the emotions in optimal functioning. Each works with emotion in its own way, and each has some wisdom about the emotional life to convey to clients. When clients are helped in therapy, it is likely that they have enhanced their emotional intelligence, aided by people who, if they themselves are not high in emotional intelligence, at least know how to raise it in others.

Phronesis

In the *Nicomachean Ethics*, Aristotle (trans. 1985) draws distinctions among *episteme*, *techne*, and *phronesis*. Each of these terms is used to designate an "intellectual virtue" or a form of knowledge. *Episteme*, scientific knowledge, is knowledge of what is universally or invariably the case. *Techne*, technical skill, involves the proficient use of *means* to achieve a set of preestablished ends. *Phronesis*, practical wisdom, has to do with ethical decision-making amid the complexities of varying everyday situations, each of which may be unique. Phronesis involves the grasping of the particularities of a concrete, real-world situation and ascertaining the means and *ends* appropriate to that situation. Sartre's example of a man faced with deciding whether to stay with his aged mother or go off to fight the Germans is the kind of dilemma requiring phronesis. But so too are the manifold mundane decisions we all face: Should I study psychology or law? Should I lecture my child or send him to his room? Should I eat a piece of chocolate cake or preserve my waistline?

Although it evolved within a very different worldview, the concept of phronesis is much akin to the modern concept of practical intelligence. Both involve a knack for making good decisions in complex everyday life situations, where general rules and formulas never precisely describe any specific real-world situation with which we are confronted.

Aristotle compares phronesis with both episteme and techne. Episteme is, in James's parlance, knowledge-about. It is universal knowledge that does not include application and does not depend on practical experience. Phronesis and techne are similar in that each comprises the kind of know-how required for the application of general knowledge to specific situations. Both require practical experience and necessarily involve knowledge-by-acquaintance. But phronesis and techne differ significantly, in that phronesis involves determining what means *and* what ends should be pursued in a given situation, whereas techne is concerned only with means. Techne is focused on expediency, whereas phronesis is concerned with both the establishment of goals and the means of realizing those goals. Technical expertise, in the form of general rules, often can formulaically generate the means of realizing a particular goal in a specific situation (for example, a recipe for baking a cherry pie). But every practical-moral decision potentially carries with it some uncertainty about how a general norm applies to a specific situation, in terms of both the ends *and* means to be pursued. A recent graduate of an assertiveness training course may adopt the ethos promulgated by many cognitive-behavior therapists, and resolve to "stand up for his rights." This cogent credo, however, does not always result in unproblematic application. Phronesis here requires not only techniques of assertiveness and some general guidelines as to their use but also the ability to select judiciously the issues and people toward which such techniques should be directed.

The example of self-assertion and defense of one's rights can be used to illustrate another characteristic of phronesis: that only in the course of applying generic guidelines to concrete situations are we able to develop the kind of understanding that gives the

guidelines practical utility. In the course of applying a rule to particular, real-world circumstances, we inevitably deepen, expand,
and modify our understanding of the rule. Without concrete
instances of application, global behavioral prescriptions tend to be
empty generalities. In the case of our assertiveness trainee, for
example, the concept of "rights" entitling assertiveness will be
somewhat abstract until his real-world experience in identifying
and defending rights enables a more complete unpacking and flesh-
ing out of the concept. He will then come to understand what it is
for him, in his particular life given his unique needs, predisposi-
tions, and life circumstances, to function assertively.

Understanding and Application

Gadamer has argued that the kind of understanding we have of
ourselves, of other people, or of any concrete expression of mental
life is analogous to Aristotle's concept of phronesis. For Gadamer
there is always a practical-moral dimension involved in understanding the actions and works of human beings, be they pieces of
literature, objects of art, or descriptions of psychological distress.
He states that in interpreting social or historical events there is
always a phronesis-like element of application to the context of the
interpreter. For some varieties of general knowledge, the application of that knowledge to concrete situations is an essential aspect
of the process of understanding.

The practice of jurisprudence illustrates this dimension of
hermeneutic understanding. In judicial hermeneutics there is
always the necessity to relate a generic law or legal principle to a
concrete, real-world situation. This process, however, does not
involve an algorithmic instantiation of specific circumstances into
a general rule, as in the case of the "laws" of natural science. Nor is
it analogous to technical reasoning. Legal principles or enacted
statutes are not mathematical formulas that yield a single solution
when a given set of values is inserted in the place of variables. In
fact, the actual content of a law cannot be divorced from how it is

interpreted and applied. The First Amendment to the U.S. Constitution guarantees freedom of speech. But the concept of freedom, as it pertains to linguistic expression, is empty until applied to concrete life situations. After years of judicial interpretation we come to understand to what conditions this freedom extends and what the limitations on it are. Thus an abstract concept is elaborated, constituted, and sometimes itself transformed by the linked processes of interpretation and application.

The particular conditions of a legal case also determine what interpretive questions we ask of the law, through what lens we view it. *Brown* v. *Board of Education of Topeka, Kansas* caused us to ask of the Fourteenth Amendment what the term *equal protection under the law* means with respect to questions of educational opportunity. The legally mandated integration of public schools was clearly not envisioned by the authors of the Fourteenth Amendment or by interpreters from sociohistorical vantage points prior to the 1950s. Earlier interpreters had sought to relate the concepts contained in the amendment to very different sets of circumstances. Today we have great difficulty imagining what meaning will be found in the "equal protection under the law" clause by future interpreters who will seek to understand it in relation to practical concerns we cannot currently envision. Practical understanding emerges only when we attempt to relate general principles to specific, concrete concerns.

Thus for both Gadamer and Aristotle, in the practical arena there is a constant tacking between general and particular, and a process of mutual influence between means and ends. And unlike technical knowledge, which consists entirely in knowing *how* to do, practical knowledge also includes knowing *what* to do.

It is only in the acting out of our various roles and identities that we develop our generalizations about them. Most of us want to be successful in our work and in our families. We have many general goals, such as being a good parent. But we discover in the course of numerous specific situations that parenting often requires choices between being on amicable terms with our children and enforcing family rules. Being a good parent may mean different, incompatible things at different times. When we try to blend being a good parent with other goals, such as being a good business person, we further realize that maximal success in all our roles is not possible. Inevitably, conflicts among goals will unfold as everyday situations develop. The reflections, decisions, and actions taken in resolving such conflicts serve both to help us discover and to better comprehend who we are and what we care about.

The psychotherapist is much involved in the development and exercise of phronesis. This is very dramatically the case when psychotherapy interacts with the legal system, as in occurrences of domestic violence. Phronesis is also very evidently called for when one conducts therapy with a client from a vastly different culture and is required to confront the cultural situatedness of the concepts and folkways of the established mental health professions.

But phronesis is called for even in the most mundane psychotherapy. Let me provide some illustration by taking two examples of technique-intensive approaches to psychotherapy: generic cognitive-behavior therapy and cognitive-behavior therapy that is administered according to the dictates of a standardized treatment manual. In the case of generic cognitive-behavior therapy, one postulate of this system is that therapy is thought of as pure techne directed toward the achievement of goals set by the client (recall Chapter Three). As cognitive-behavior therapy defines psychotherapy, goal setting—an extratechnical activity—must be outside the process of therapy. Yet the cognitive-behavior therapist and the client must, as a practical matter, engage in some conversation about goals, in order to specify them. The conversation may be short, as in "I'm afraid to leave the house. Please help me conquer my fear." But what is presented by the client to the therapist may instead be diffuse and inchoate: "I'm feeling uneasy, unhappy, and I don't know why." This addressing of goals may, in fact, not end after an initial discussion and assessment, but rather be continuous throughout therapy. Yet whenever the deliberation and discussion of therapeutic objectives occurs, for however long, it involves some activity of the therapist not comprehended by science or technique. When the cognitive-behavior therapist discusses with the client what behaviors the client wishes modified, the therapist is engaged, to some degree, in a contractual negotiation, not in the application of scientific technology. In practice, the therapist will be doing a number of things in connection with setting therapeutic goals: sifting through what the client presents using some mixture of the *DSM* and what the client is asking for, while concurrently drawing upon some store of knowledge derived from clinical experience (much of which is tacit) about which therapeutic endeavors are likely to be worthwhile.

Even those simple cases involving clients who merely want to achieve the freedom to move about in the world, the agoraphobics, are not always so simple that they involve nothing but technique. A woman I treated with a standardized protocol (Barlow & Craske, 1988) presented complicated challenges to therapy that are not inevitable but certainly are not unusual. The patient in question had presented symptoms of panic and agoraphobia. She manifested what is unfelicitously termed comorbidity (that is, she had problems beyond those specified in the primary diagnosis). She had additional phobias and showed some generalized anxiety along with some mild depression. She was also rather submissive and acquiescent with her husband and children. She had submerged herself in other people. Most of her pleasures were vicarious. Progress in conquering her fears led to disruptions in her family. As my client increased her freedom, she exercised theretofore unavailable options to change her role in the family. There were points at which it seemed that she risked losing many of the benefits of her life as it had existed before therapy. My dialogue with her centered around such subjects as whether therapy should be continued, the inevitable trade-offs occasioned by major life changes, and the worth and viability of various life scenarios.

There are few formulas for addressing these kinds of concerns. Therapists enact various roles in such situations. Some therapists are directive; some are nondirective. Some therapists have answers;

some only raise questions. I served as my client's partner in conversation, not because I was the most qualified person to do so or had techniques that would resolve her dilemmas, but because I was there at the time and understood her particular circumstances and concerns in those various and important ways that therapists do.

What the therapist has to offer in many therapeutic situations is neither science nor art. It is more like pedagogical companionship, accompanied, at its best, by wisdom, judgment, discernment. The role of therapist as adviser, guide, or partner in Socratic dialogue will always be a component of psychotherapy. This much I believe to be certain. What is uncertain is what capacities and conceptualizations therapists of the future will bring to these ministrations that occur on that very personal terrain of the lifeworld, within the context of the sociocultural Background, where the cognition is hot and suffused with emotion, where choices have significant practical consequences, where fact and value are joined.

Chapter Seven

Psychotherapy and Contemporary Controversies

Psychotherapy is at a crossroads. The first three-quarters of this century was the era of originators, founders of a school of therapy: Freud, Rogers, Wolpe, Ellis, Beck, Perls, and Lazarus. It was an extraordinary period, marked by invention that bore the stamp of genius. But this time in the history of psychotherapy seems to have passed. Over the last two decades there has been a paucity of innovation, either in theory or technique. The field has entered a period of consolidation, in which research activity has been focused on refinement of existing methods. Competition among rival schools has receded during an era marked by eclecticism, ecumenicism, integrationism, and theoretical pluralism.

Despite this relative internal harmony, these are not tranquil times for psychotherapy. Though there has been a significant increase in public acceptance of psychotherapy (VandenBos, 1996), clinicians currently are involved in a desperate battle to retain a position in the health care firmament. The broad-based national effort to curb health care expenditures has rendered uncertain the futures of all health care professionals. Because their activities are comparatively esoteric, psychotherapists have been pressed especially hard to explain and justify what they do. In 1993 and 1994 the American Psychological Association embarked on the most aggressive and energetic lobbying effort in its history, in the process continually warning its members that psychotherapy was in real danger of being removed from the register of legitimate health care procedures and therefore being made ineligible for reimbursement by underwriting third parties. Extinction, it was implied, inevitably would follow.

127

Although an economically driven metamorphosis of the huge fee-for-service outpatient psychotherapy industry already has begun, the disappearance of psychotherapy, as defined broadly, seems highly unlikely. The various technologies and pedagogies of self-transformation are simply too integral to contemporary culture to vanish, in the absence of some wider social transmutation. We do not know what form the psychotherapy of the future will take. Yet it will be here in some form.

Hard times are, of course, nothing new for psychotherapy. From its very beginning psychotherapy struggled to achieve acceptance and legitimacy. Misgivings about psychotherapy and its associated theories of human behavior have been with us from the very beginning. Karl Krauss, the Viennese social critic and a contemporary of Freud, referred to psychoanalysis as "that spiritual disease of which it considers itself to be the cure" (cited in Janik & Toulmin, 1973, p. 75). Another man of Freud's time, the always incisive Max Weber (1907/1978), bemoaned the egoistic, hedonistic ideology he believed to be implicit in psychoanalysis. He was early in a long line of individuals that has included Kingsley Davis, Philip Rieff, Christopher Lasch, Alasdair MacIntyre, and Robert Bellah. These social philosophers and sociologists have enunciated the same essential theme: psychotherapy as a problematic feature of modernity, one whose ideas and practices are inimical to the communal and moral penchants of older, traditional, and more salutary forms of social organization.

While the sociocultural critique of psychotherapy was evaluating therapeutic worldviews and finding them defective, another kind of challenge was issued to psychotherapy. From within the disciplines at the foundation of the mental health professions, psychotherapy was called on to prove its worth by an objective demonstration of efficacy. It was Hans Eysenck (1952) who began the empirical critique of psychotherapy with data indicating that patients in psychotherapy showed no greater relief from symptoms than those receiving no treatment. For several decades, especially in academic departments, skeptics regarding the efficacy of therapy abounded.

Their numbers have diminished greatly in the wake of copious research substantiating psychotherapy's effectiveness (Lipsey & Wilson, 1993; Seligman, 1995; Smith, Glass, & Miller, 1980).[24]

Research on the outcomes of psychotherapy, while legitimizing therapy as an effective treatment, concurrently has raised questions about some of the institution's most widely held assumptions. One of these is that extensive academic education coupled with considerable professional training and experience make for the best therapists. Another is that different therapeutic approaches—for example, psychodynamic versus cognitive-behavioral—produce distinguishable outcomes. The results of empirical research have tended to be at considerable variance with these assumptions. Although psychotherapy can ameliorate a wide array of psychological problems and psychiatric disorders, there are few unambiguous demonstrations that any form of therapy is superior to any other, at least with most of the problems brought to therapists.[25] Training and clinical experience bear a highly uncertain relation to therapeutic effectiveness.[26] These findings have invited the conclusion that psychotherapy owes its effects to mechanisms that can be mobilized without benefit of an advanced degree. These mechanisms, it is argued, may be common to all forms of psychotherapy.[27]

If we were to conclude from the published empirical research that most therapists are overqualified and that whatever a therapist is inclined to do in therapy is likely to have a beneficial effect on clients, the myriad headlines and malpractice suits would supply convincing refutation.[28] The admixture of intimacy and the capacity for influence that lies at the heart of the therapist-patient relationship makes therapy a high-stakes endeavor wherein professional misconduct or misjudgment may have devastating consequences. The media have ensured a high degree of public awareness of these unfortunate aspects of clinical practice. The public is becoming aware, as well, of the potentially harmful effects of certain therapeutic ideologies. Courts are beginning to find against therapists who have facilitated patients' false or distorted recollections of abuse during childhood. The fractured families, the jail sentences, and the destruction of lives that have resulted are another reminder of the power of psychotherapy and the seemingly limitless credulity of some therapists and clients (Crews, 1994a, 1994b; Sileo, 1995).

Psychotherapy: Some Observations and Recommendations

In the pages that follow, I extend my analysis from the previous chapters to comment on some issues central to theory and practice in the mental health professions. I attempt few systematic arguments in defense of the speculations offered.

Psychotherapy Should Be a House with Many Mansions

As we have seen, psychotherapy can be regarded from many different vantage points and conceptualized in many different fashions. It is, at once, all of the following: social institution, applied science, interpretive humanistic study, technology of personal development, and source and mirror of cultural metamorphosis. The evolution of psychotherapy is both the development of a field of expert knowledge and a process by which a culture interprets and defines itself. Psychotherapy is a vehicle through which we not only shape ourselves but also derive our standards and sensibilities. It is a kind of cultural laboratory in which various views of human nature, models of interpersonal relations, and systems of values are put forth and evaluated. The diversity of the psychotherapies has been, in this respect, of some use to us. We have had opportunity to subject many ideals and many models of conduct to the practical tests of social applicability that psychotherapy allows. We have learned from psychotherapy that open marriages are good in theory but do not work in practice. We have learned that most sexual preferences are not malleable and that tolerance of gay and lesbian lifestyles is the best policy. We are in the process of learning that being overweight should not be regarded inevitably as a sign of sloth or self-indulgence. Soon we likely will know whether or not the mind does such magical things as hide from itself many of the tortures and abuses experienced in childhood.

Human beings have created art, literature, morals, jurisprudence, and many other cultural devices in the course of efforts to depict, understand, regulate, and transform the existence into which we are thrown. The discourses inherent in these varied social and experiential forms, as Dilthey hinted a century ago, cannot be translated into simpler idioms. To render life fully and comprehensively, we need multiple levels of analysis: biochemical, physiological, experiential, behavioral, sociological, evaluative, and aesthetic. Psychotherapy, being a vast, multifaceted cultural project directed at the systematic transformation, facilitation, and comprehension of human lives, must assimilate and make contact with the manifold frames of reference that human beings use to both understand and change themselves.

Thus far no approach to psychotherapy has won out in the contest of therapeutic efficacy, although for problems of living that are specific and circumscribed, the therapeutic methods that are closest to common sense seem to possess an advantage. For example, confronting fears of external objects seems to reduce those fears more than does exploring the similarities between feelings for one's therapist and for one's parents. Preventing people from compulsively washing their hands works better to eliminate the response than having them get in touch with their "inner child." Yet it is much too early in the game to start declaring large bodies of thought obsolete and spurious, or to start burning the books describing approaches whose efficacy is not yet substantiated by controlled empirical studies. Unrestrained scientism today would vanquish all approaches to classifying psychopathology save that of the American Psychiatric Association's diagnostic manual, a book whose earlier editions would have been committed to the flames by scientistic behaviorist zealots of the 1960s and 1970s. From that earlier historical vantage point, it was the disease model of psychopathology and any trait-based classification system that had been proved unscientific.

Psychotherapy Is Vulnerable to Sophistry

One of the things we have learned from psychotherapy is that, in the realm of human affairs, skepticism is almost always warranted. We have learned this, in part, because psychotherapy and psychotherapists frequently have manifested extraordinary credulity and folly. Psychotherapists have been highly receptive to bizarre and wacky ideas. Psychotherapy has given us primal screams, the thesis of universal abuse and victimization, regression to past lives, and electric shocks administered to the testicles of homosexuals. Why this should be has, I believe, to do with a need, on the part of both therapists and clients, to transcend the mundane.

Consider the psychotherapist. Every day of his professional life he is asked questions to which he does not have the answers and is confronted with problems he does not understand and cannot ameliorate. His patients assume he knows more than he does and constantly give evidence of their imprudent expectations. Most therapists are humanitarians, but they cannot be as helpful to their clients as they would wish. The problems brought to them are too recalcitrant, and the art and technology they practice too weak to transform personality and character. The gap between therapeutic knowledge and effectiveness, on the one hand, and the needs and hopes of patients, on the other, can demoralize therapists.

When a therapist encounters new, highly touted theories and methods that offer straightforward explanations of poorly understood and refractory disorders, and methods that offer to dramatically expand her healing power, the allure is palpable. What was complex can be made simple. Feelings of inadequacy are replaced with those of confidence and power. Sometimes new therapeutic remedies are employed as panaceas. New ideas and theories can become dogma and bigotry.

An example of this kind of development is the recent enthusiasm for using hypnosis and other suggestive techniques to recover memories of childhood sexual abuse[29] that are alleged to have been repressed. A related phenomenon is the increasing number of individuals diagnosed with dissociative identity disorder (multiple personality), a dysfunction once thought to be exceedingly rare. We can perhaps add to this list therapists who specialize in uncovering ritual satanic abuse and those who treat the aftereffects of abduction by extraterrestrials. What all these developments share is a credulity toward the unordinary and a view that the mind possesses mysterious powers that can be channeled by the ministrations of one who understands their operation. The therapist in these arenas functions much as a magician or an exorcist, healing personae more glamorous and powerful than those associated with the standard fare of psychotherapy.

Patients as well as therapists feel the desire for potent, quasi-magical therapeutic nostrums. The various needs people have to experience drama in their lives and to believe in mysterious entities are well documented (Sagan, 1995). Many patients also want to trust in a better tomorrow, to believe that life is not so unremittingly hard as their current battles with psychopathology would suggest. Many of us would choose salvation and transfiguration over the meager solaces of self-awareness and stoical resolve. Given the roles that psychotherapy plays in society, it is not surprising that those needs and preferences are acted out in treatment.

The therapeutic situation is a fertile breeding ground for sophistry and misconception. Most often the therapist works in isolation. Her activity is neither observed nor supervised. She receives feedback primarily from her clients. Many therapists do not read the scientific literature (Beutler, Williams, Wakefield, & Entwistle, 1995), often preferring to acquire information from trade books, workshops, and association newsletters. Over the course of their careers, they become further and further removed from whatever critical tradition they encountered in their graduate training. They tend to drift toward the kinds of clients and methods that enhance their feelings of professional competence. They may achieve real or apparent success with clients even when their methods are based on falsehoods.

The Misuse of Hermeneutics

Skepticism and critical thinking are prophylactics against the susceptibility of psychotherapy to assimilate false beliefs and injurious practices. Psychotherapy is a profession in need of a critical tradition that can be implemented in a way that ameliorates the problems cited previously.

The great virtue of scientific modes of thought is that they represent one critical tradition that many workers in the field have been trained in and know how to put into practice. To date, science is the only critical tradition to have been successfully implemented within the mental health professions. Many fields outside the sciences—history, law, and philosophy, to name a few—have a rich heritage of subjecting ideas to exacting scrutiny. Yet thus far, attempts by psychotherapy to borrow from other traditions have been less than successful.

As an example, most psychotherapists who have sought to import hermeneutic conceptions into psychotherapy have tended to deform those conceptions in a postmodern direction—so as to make them resemble epistemological relativism and social constructionism. The postmodern trend within psychotherapy opposes attempts to privilege any therapeutic narrative and aims to dispense with truth as a criterion for the various conclusions reached by client and therapist over a course of therapeutic treatment (Held, 1995).

Hermeneutic models applied to psychotherapy have stimulated the abandonment of any attempt to establish criteria for the evaluation of therapeutic interpretations other than those of internal coherence, aesthetic appeal, or therapeutic efficacy (Sass and Woolfolk, 1988). For both Schafer and Spence, as well as for various nonpsychoanalytic "constructivist" psychotherapists (White & Epston, 1990; Neimeyer, 1993) there is little authority or "truth" an interpretation can possess beyond its power to reframe events so that people come to feel better about themselves or to act in "healthier" ways. As the constructivists would put it, the client's problem is "restoried," or made part of a new narrative that has the power to improve the client's problem. Within a constructivist scheme this is about all there is to therapy: finding the right narrative, the one that makes the problem better.

To be concerned only with the efficacy of an interpretation and not with its truth or validity, ultimately will lead either to therapeutic cynicism or to the collapse of therapeutic authority and credibility. Therapeutic interpretations whose only claim to validity is that they make us feel good or help us behave more effectively will do neither if we, as clients, come to understand that the interpretations were fabricated for this specific reason alone and have no other claim to authority. Why should we believe such narratives, considering that they were made up just for us and have no plausibility save that, if we believe, we will feel better? I might feel happier if I think I am going to live forever, but I will not be convinced of my immortality entirely on that basis. I will believe it to be true only on some basis beyond my wanting and wishing it. In the practical world of everyday life, desire is neither necessary nor sufficient for attributions of truth. In fact, a large part of any personal or cultural system of belief involves contrasts between what we *want* to be the case and what actually *is* the case.

Constructivist psychotherapy is inevitably self-undermining. It requires the therapist either to misrepresent the basis of therapeutic pronouncements, in order that they be believed, or to disclose their basis and ensure that they will not be believed.[30]

The constructivist therapies that call themselves hermeneutic but dispense with the truth criterion and embrace relativism, are fundamentally unhermeneutic. Ironically, both Gadamer and Dilthey aimed to expand the number of disciplines in which truth claims could be made.[31] Dilthey sought to establish interpretive methods for a set of sciences that could seek and attain the truth about the social, cultural, and psychological dimensions of human existence. Gadamer attempted to demonstrate the historical situatedness of the human sciences and to show that understanding the actions of human beings involves uncovering truth, but truth that is constrained by a sociocultural horizon, truth that can be identified only from a particular vantage point. In the aftermath of Thomas Kuhn's work, many philosophers of science believe that the physical sciences have similar epistemological limits and provisionality—that they discover not objective truth but true accounts within the conceptual horizon of a given hermeneutic framework. Neither in physics nor in psychotherapy does hermeneutic thought imply abandoning the attempt to establish the validity of our ideas.

Another case of psychotherapy's importing hermeneutic ideas but employing them in the service of practices that run counter to the main currents of hermeneutic thought is the appropriation of hermeneutic ideas by therapies that rely extensively on the client's introspection—for example, psychoanalysis. In psychoanalysis, self-knowledge becomes equated with a highly elaborated knowledge of one's inner spaces. Yet almost the entire thrust of hermeneutic thought is away from inwardness and toward the outer, public sphere.

In fact, hermeneutics views all social knowledge, even self-knowledge, as knowledge of public events. Introspection is thought to be unreliable. When an individual tries, as Dilthey (1976, p. 176) puts it, "to hold fast and grasp his states of mind by turning his attention upon himself, then the narrow limits of such an introspective method of self-knowledge show themselves; only his actions and creations and the effects they have on others teach man about himself." For hermeneutic thinkers, as with existentialists (for example, Sartre[32]) and cognitive-behaviorists, it is action that is primary (Woolfolk & Sass, 1988). A truly hermeneutic conception of self-knowledge would not be based on the dubious method of introspection (Nisbett & Wilson, 1977) but rather on analysis of our actions. The cognitive-behavioral approaches of Albert Bandura and Daryl Bem are true to the hermeneutic tradition in that Bem (1972) tells us that we infer our attitudes from observation of our actions and Bandura (1986) claims that our sense of self-efficacy is not much affected by stories other people tell us, but rather by our conduct,[33] the behavior we engage in and the consequences that ensue from it. We believe ourselves to possess those qualities we observe ourselves demonstrating, both to ourselves and to other people.

Therapy Should Be Rational—Not Scientistic

Therapists need to approach their work with the careful inductive logic, the reliance on empirical observation, and the skepticism of the scientist. Yet as therapists we cannot function entirely as scientists. In the practical sphere of everyday life our actions cannot be based on formal scientific experimentation. Each of us has a stock of knowledge upon which our actions are predicated. Some of what we know, as Paul Meehl (1997) suggested recently, we do not need systematic scientific studies to validate. Wine glasses break when you drop them on tile floors, and most people will come to dislike you if you are constantly cruel to them. Other beliefs we hold could never be tested because they involve numerous complex and confounded variables. Yet we cannot get by without knowledge of this sort, knowledge that we do not or cannot test scientifically. Much of what therapy is about is refining and critiquing this kind of knowledge, attaining what I have labeled, after Aristotle, practical wisdom.

We also cannot exist without the values and preferences that constitute our personhood. Without the motivation and direction that our tastes and ethics provide, there would be nothing to our lives, no actions for scientific or practical knowledge to direct. To engage the normative dimensions of clients' lives satisfactorily, the therapist must draw from cultural sources other than the technologies of contemporary behavioral and medical science. What those other sources are or should be we in the mental health field and in the culture at large are in the process of deciding. The endeavor merits our most sincere and scrupulous efforts.

Notes

Chapter One

1. The effects of psychoanalysis on midcentury sexual mores and child-rearing practices are straightforward examples.
2. *Cura animarum,* a Latin expression used in the medieval Roman Catholic Church, referred to "the sustaining and curative treatment of persons in those matters that reach beyond the requirements of the animal life" (McNeill, 1951, p. vii). The expression usually is translated as "cure of souls," although the Latin *cura* also denotes "care," as in "curator." The cure of souls was an aspect of priestly responsibility related to *casuistry,* the determination of right and wrong in matters of conduct (Nelson, 1981).

Chapter Two

3. I prefer to remain agnostic on the question of postmodernity. There is an oft-observed tendency of people in every era to believe they stand on some great historical divide. There is also a recent infatuation in intellectual circles with the prefix *post,* as in "postempirical," "poststructural." When pressed, I incline toward the views of Giddens (1991) and Wellmer (1991), who see the persistence and evolution of the basic themes of modernity into the present time.
4. Although both Marxism and psychoanalysis currently appear to be fading in influence, each has weathered various declines

in the past only to renew itself, sometimes in modified form, in a different geographical or cultural context.

5. Hume was not, of course, the first ethical skeptic. The Greek sophists, whom Plato was so concerned to refute, questioned whether ethical judgments could be "validated" on any objective basis. Thrasymachus, who appears in the *Republic*, suggests that morality is simply a matter of personal preference. What we like we call "good," and what we dislike we label "bad."

6. I am describing a phenomenon sociologists call medicalization, the process through which everyday life comes under medical influence and supervision. Through medicalization "nonmedical problems become defined and treated as medical problems, usually in terms of illnesses or disorders" (Conrad, 1992, p. 209). Examples of phenomena that have become medicalized are learning disabilities in children, child abuse, overeating, compulsive gambling, and menstrual discomfort.

7. I refer here to Heidegger's infamous Nazi period, which most authorities see as closely related to the aspirations of his philosophy and his antipathy for the modern age (Wolin, 1991).

Chapter Three

8. Although clinical eclecticism (a therapist's borrowing techniques from different approaches to therapy) is extremely common, attempts to render consistent the theories on which the multifarious schools of therapy are based have not achieved resounding success (Lazarus, 1995; Messer & Winokur, 1980; Wilson, 1995). Some have argued that theoretical differences among therapies are unimportant and that it is the procedural commonalities shared by different therapies that effect improvement via mechanisms that are not accounted for in their underlying theories (Frank, 1973; Goldfried, 1980).

9. According to Szasz (1978), correlative with the myth of mental illness is the "myth of psychotherapy." On this account

psychotherapy is an activity that has nothing in common with the practice of medicine, which is a true applied science. Psychotherapy is, for Szasz, a nonscientific rhetorical endeavor in which the therapist attempts to persuade the patient to adopt conduct or attitudes consistent with some secularly derived system of "therapeutic" values. Hence, psychotherapy is conceived not as a form of applied science but as applied ethics—an entirely *moral* enterprise.

10. Of course the therapist might try to convert the client to a "healthy" set of values without explaining the rationale of health promotion. Convincing the client to "believe" on some ostensible basis other than salutary effect, however, would seem a cynical and futile undertaking for all therapists except those who could play the missionary with sincere conviction.

Chapter Four

11. For both Plato and Aristotle, *sophrosyne* is associated with the rational control of desires, and awareness of one's civic duties. In translations of their writings *sophrosyne* is usually rendered as "temperance."

12. Gray's "Elegy" is a complex meditation on fate and fortune. It reminds us of the crucial role of chance in each person's life. The poet contemplates the humble denizens of a rural graveyard "far from the madding crowd," who, but for circumstance, might have become great personages—for example, Miltons or Cromwells.

13. The term *Geisteswissenschaften* frequently is translated as "social sciences" or "human sciences." As Dilthey and other nineteenth-century scholars understood the term, it subsumed some domains we currently would place within the humanities as well as those that fall into our current category "social sciences." The *Geisteswissenschaften* included not only psychology and anthropology but also philology and aesthetics (Makkreel, 1975).

14. Although Schleiermacher did seek a kind of reconstruction of the author's mental world and intent, defined very broadly, this objective was not to be achieved solely by nor limited to empathic understanding. Schleiermacher's view was that the interpreter has access to a range of information not available to the author. Therefore, "[t]he task [of interpretation] is to be formulated as follows: 'To understand the text at first as well as and then even better than its author' " (Schleiermacher, 1819/1985, p. 83).

15. Dilthey's program (1976, 1989) for the human sciences actually relies on neither empathy nor introspection, nor is it opposed to all physicalistic or mechanistic explanation of human conduct. Dilthey, in fact, advocated a multidisciplinary approach to the study of behavior that encompassed not only interpretive understanding of meanings and purposes but also the causal relationships between biological underpinnings and behavior. In his view, neither understanding nor explanation was sufficient to give the kind of comprehensive account required by the complexities of human conduct.

16. The attempt to hermeneuticize psychoanalysis has not been welcomed by all psychoanalysts. Criticism of hermeneutic perspectives has been frequent and spirited (Edelston, 1988; Grünbaum, 1990; Steiner, 1995). Today only a minority of psychoanalysts are solidly in the hermeneutic camp.

17. Schafer's views are similar to those of the psychoanalyst George Klein (1976), who argued that the Freudian metapsychology is incompatible with the clinical theory of psychoanalysis. The clinical theory refers both to the psychoanalytic theory of personality dynamics, especially the theory of psychological defense, and to the theory of psychoanalytic technique. A principal feature that distinguishes the clinical theory from the metapsychology is its teleological language, which describes the activities of the psyche in terms of motives, goals, and purposes. Klein advocates eliminating the metapsychology, an operation he calls a theorectomy.

Chapter Five

18. The Latin expression is translated as "after that, therefore because of that" and refers to the logical error of inferring that event A causes event B simply because A occurs before B. *Post hoc ergo propter hoc* is a special case of the fallacy of the "false cause" (Copi, 1961). A related instance of the false cause fallacy familiar to behavioral scientists is that of inferring causation from mere correlation.

19. The analysis of self-understanding does not assume that the self is a cohesive or unitary entity, or that there is a "true" self that one can discover. I do assume that people form cognitive representations of self and draw conclusions about what and who they are, what they wish to do, what they are able to do, and what they are likely to do.

20. B. F. Skinner was a notable exception to this rule. He used behaviorist terminology to characterize his activities as a scientist and employed operant conditioning techniques to maximize his scientific output (Skinner, 1983).

21. We can test the empirical assumptions that underlie any value judgment. Value judgments are often predicated on "factual" assumptions that can be tested empirically. Yet there is a normative, subjective residual in any evaluation that resists complete translation into scientific hypotheses.

Chapter Six

22. Cognition and affect are closely related, although the degree to which cognition and affect are independent is a matter of some debate (Lazarus, 1991; Zajonc, 1984). Emotions are, perhaps, best conceived as integrations of complex responses occurring at many levels of the organism, for example, cognitive, expressive, physiological (Leventhal, 1979). One recent attempt to place emotions on dimensions (Watson & Clark, 1984)

suggests that every emotion reveals whether we feel "good" or "bad" about the current state of affairs.

23. Aristotle describes three forms of "belittlement" that provoke anger: spite, contempt, and insult. His analysis goes on to indicate that such provocations must be perceived as intentional and unjustified to result in the emotion of anger.

Chapter Seven

24. There is considerable disagreement among scholars about what has been established by research on psychotherapy. Most would agree that bringing a psychological problem to a therapist is more likely to result in its amelioration than taking no action or seeking some informal remedy. Some contend that most forms of therapy are effective with most disorders, producing improvement that is practically meaningful to clients (Howard, 1995). Others argue that therapy generally produces improvement that is statistically superior to that found in control groups, but that the improvement often is not consequential (Jacobson, 1995). Still others would argue that some approaches have been proven effective with certain disorders (usually cognitive-behavioral methods with specific, unitary disorders) whereas other approaches await adequate testing and, therefore, remain unvalidated (Wilson, 1995).

25. Neither of the two most famous studies that pitted different forms of therapy against each other (Sloane, Staples, Cristol, Yorkston, & Whipple, 1975; Elkin et al., 1989) yielded a clear-cut victor. Comparisons of therapeutic impact across studies (meta-analyses) have tended to favor cognitive-behavioral approaches somewhat, although the logical problems in aggregating data from different, sometimes incomparable, studies may impugn this conclusion.

26. Again views differ as to what the research literature demonstrates regarding the value of training and clinical experience.

One notorious study failed to show experienced clinicians as more effective than untrained nonprofessionals (Strupp & Hadley, 1979). Aggregate findings from different studies have caused some reviewers (Dawes, 1994; Christensen & Jacobson, 1993) to minimize the importance of training and experience, whereas others find some evidence that experience and training are positively related to outcome (Lambert & Bergin, 1994). My own view is that the matter is far from settled and will be difficult to settle. Counterfactuals are notoriously hard to prove. The inductive logic of standard experimental designs is such that the null hypothesis, "Experience, training, or both make no difference in outcome," cannot be confirmed. Both conceptual clarity and appropriately designed studies have been lacking in this area, making the potential for confusion and demagoguery high. What does seem to be occurring is that, perhaps for reasons largely economic, HMOs and managed care corporations are happy to have psychotherapy administered by master's level clinicians in lieu of clinicians holding doctorates.

27. Jerome Frank (1961, 1971) was the first to describe what many subsequent writers have called the "common factors" of diverse forms of therapy. According to this view, all therapy involves a supportive relationship with a therapist, the opportunity to disclose one's difficulties to a sympathetic listener, encouragement and reassurance, and the restoration of hope.

28. It is well established that the conditions of some patients in psychotherapy deteriorate. In research studies, rates of deterioration are typically higher in treatment groups than in control groups. Psychotherapy results in improvement for most clients, but produces decrements in others (Lambert & Bergin, 1994). Careless treatment, poor matching of clients and treatments, emotional disturbance on the part of the therapist, and overly aggressive breaking down of client defenses have been implicated as potential contributors to negative treatment outcomes (Beutler, Machado, & Neufeldt, 1994). Both malfeasance, (for example, sexual misconduct) and negligence (for example,

failure to assess suicidal proclivities) can also damage clients (Campbell, 1994; Sherman, 1993).

29. The sexual abuse of children is a prevalent, grievous moral and social problem the effects of which are only beginning to be understood. Yet many psychotherapists with no legitimate knowledge of the problem claim expert status. A thorough discussion of this topic is beyond the scope of this writing, and I would not contend that all that has been done in the name of exploring the sexual abuse patients have experienced in childhood has been pernicious. Yet the evidence clearly points to the implantation of suggestions in some cases and to widespread naïveté, ignorance, and intellectual negligence among many who are believers in the recovery of repressed memories. Numerous lives have been damaged unnecessarily. Currently the courts as well as the scientific community are in the process of sorting out these issues.

30. Barbara Held (1995) has suggested still another possibility— that the postmodern therapy might "sneak in" some unacknowledged foundationalism, for example, and thereby undermine itself by resting on a metatheoretical contradiction.

31. Gadamer is no relativist. He writes that human beings require "the sense of what is feasible, what is possible, what is correct . . ." (1975a, p. xxv). He advances hermeneutics as "a discipline of questioning and research, a discipline that guarantees truth" (1975a, p. 447).

32. "A man is nothing else but the sum of his actions," Sartre (1946/1949, p. 41) writes.

33. Bandura (1986) lists four sources of self-knowledge about one's efficacy: performance attainments, vicarious experiences from observing the actions of others, verbal persuasion and other forms of social influence, and physiological states. Research has shown performance attainments to provide the most influential source of efficacy information.

References

Albert, E. A., Denise, T. C., & Peterfreund, S. P. (1980). *Great traditions in ethics* (4th ed.). New York: Van Nostrand Reinhold.

Aristotle. (1961). *Poetics* (S. H. Butcher, Trans.). New York: Hill & Wang.

Aristotle. (1985). *Nicomachean ethics* (T. H. Irwin, Trans.). Indianapolis: Hackett.

Aristotle. (1991). *The art of rhetoric* (H. C. Lawson-Tancred, Trans.). London: Penguin.

Augustine. (1992). *Confessions* (Book X). Reprinted in V. J. Bourke, *Augustine's love of wisdom: An introspective philosophy*. West Lafayette, IN: Purdue University Press.

Ayer, A. J. (1946). *Language, truth and logic*. New York: Dover.

Bandura, A. (1977). *Social learning theory*. Upper Saddle River, NJ: Prentice-Hall.

Bandura, A. (1986). *Social foundations of thought and action: A social cognitive theory*. Upper Saddle River, NJ: Prentice-Hall.

Bargh, J. A. (1995, August). *The wise unconscious: Intention, automation, and social behavior*. Paper presented at the annual meeting of the American Psychological Association, New York.

Barlow, D. H., & Craske, M. G. (1988). *Mastery of your anxiety and panic*. Albany, NY: Graywind Publications.

Barthes, R. (1977). *Image, music, text* (S. Heath, Trans.). New York: Hill & Wang.

Baumeister, R. F. (1986). *Identity: Cultural change and the struggle for self*. New York: Oxford University Press.

Bell, D. (1973). *The coming of post-industrial society: A venture in social forecasting*. New York: Basic Books.

Bellah, R. N., Madsen, R., Sullivan, W. M., Swidler, A., & Tipton, S. M. (1985). *Habits of the heart*. Berkeley: University of California Press.

Bem, D. J. (1972). Self-perception theory. In L. Berkowitz (Ed.), *Advances in experimental social psychology* (Vol. 6, pp. 2–62). New York: Academic Press.

Berger, P. L., Berger, B., & Kellner, H. (1973). *The homeless mind*. New York: Random House.

Berger, P. L., & Kellner, H. (1981). *Sociology reinterpreted*. Garden City, NY: Anchor Press/Doubleday.

Berger, P. L., & Luckmann, T. (1966). *The social construction of reality.* New York: Doubleday.

Bergin, A. E. (1980). Psychotherapy and religious values. *Journal of Consulting and Clinical Psychology, 48,* 95–105.

Bergin, A. E. (1985). Proposed values for guiding and evaluating counseling and psychotherapy. *Counseling and Values, 29,* 99–116.

Bergin, A. E. (1991). Values and religious issues in psychotherapy and mental health. *American Psychologist, 46,* 394–403.

Bergin, A. E., & Garfield, S. L. (Eds.). (1994). *Handbook of psychotherapy and behavior change* (4th ed.). New York: Wiley.

Beutler, L. E., & Bergan, J. (1991). Value change in counseling and psychotherapy: A search for scientific credibility. *Journal of Counseling Psychology, 38,* 16–24.

Beutler, L. E., Machado, P. P. P., & Neufeldt, S. A. (1994). Therapist variables. In A. E. Bergin & S. L. Garfield (Eds.), *Handbook of psychotherapy and behavior change* (4th ed., pp. 229–269). New York: Wiley.

Beutler, L. E., Williams, R. E., Wakefield, P. J., & Entwistle, S. R. (1995). Bridging scientist and practitioner perspectives in clinical psychology. *American Psychologist, 50,* 984–994.

Bourdieu, P. (1977). *Outline of a theory of practice* (R. Nice, Trans.). New York: Cambridge University Press.

Bourdieu, P. (1990). *The logic of practice* (R. Nice, Trans.). Stanford, CA: Stanford University Press.

Brinton, C. (1950). *Ideas and men: The story of Western thought.* Upper Saddle River, NJ: Prentice-Hall.

Bubner, R. (1981). *Modern German philosophy.* Cambridge: Cambridge University Press.

Buss, D. M. (1991). Evolutionary personality psychology. *Annual Review of Psychology, 42,* 459–491.

Butt, M. M. (1992). *Psychology, sin, and society: An essay on the triumvirate of psychology, religion, and democracy.* Lanham, MD: University Press of America.

Campbell, J. (1968). *The hero with a thousand faces* (2nd ed.). Princeton, NJ: Princeton University Press.

Campbell, T. W. (1994). Psychotherapy and malpractice exposure. *American Journal of Forensic Psychology, 12,* 5–41.

Camus, A. (1960). *The myth of Sisyphus and other essays* (J. O'Brien, Trans.). New York: Vintage Books.

Carr, D. (1986). *Time, narrative, and history.* Bloomington: Indiana University Press.

Christensen, A., & Jacobson, N. S. (1993). Who or what can do psychotherapy: The status and challenge of nonprofessional therapies. *Psychological Science, 5,* 8–14.

Conrad, P. (1992). Medicalization and social control. *Annual Review of Sociology, 18,* 209–232.

Copi, I. M. (1961). *Introduction to logic.* New York: Macmillan.

Crews, F. (1994a, November 17). The revenge of the repressed (Part I). *New York Review of Books,* pp. 54–60.

Crews, F. (1994b, December 1). The revenge of the repressed (Part II). *New York Review of Books,* pp. 49–58.

Crites, S. (1971). The narrative quality of experience. *Journal of the American Academy of Religion, 39,* 391–411.

Cushman, P. (1995). *Constructing the self, constructing America: A cultural history of psychotherapy.* Reading, MA: Addison-Wesley.

Cutter, F. (1996). Virtual psychotherapy? *PsychNews International: An Online Publication, 1,* 1–9.

Danto, A. C. (1968). *Analytical philosophy of history.* Cambridge: Cambridge University Press.

Danto, A. C. (1985). *Narration and knowledge.* New York: Columbia University Press.

Dawes, R. M. (1994). *House of cards.* New York: Free Press.

Dewey, J. (1922). *Human nature and conduct: An introduction to social psychology.* London: Allen and Unwin.

Dewey, J. (1938). *Logic: The theory of inquiry.* New York: Henry Holt.

Dicks, H. V. (1950). In search of our proper ethic. *British Journal of Medical Psychology, 23,* 1–14.

Dihle, A. (1982). *The theory of will in classical antiquity.* Berkeley: University of California Press.

Dilthey, W. (1976). *Selected writings* (H. P. Rickman, Ed. and Trans.). Cambridge: Cambridge University Press.

Dilthey, W. (1989). *Selected works* (Vol. 1; R. A. Makkreel & F. Rodi, Eds.; R. A. Makkreel, M. Neville, & F. Schreiner, Trans.). Princeton, NJ: Princeton University Press.

Doherty, W. J. (1995). *Soul searching: Why psychotherapy must promote moral responsibility.* New York: Basic Books.

Dreyfus, H. L. (1991). *Being-in-the-world: A commentary on Heidegger's Being and Time, Division I.* Cambridge, MA: MIT Press.

Edelston, M. (1988). *Psychoanalysis: A theory in crisis.* Chicago: University of Chicago Press.

Edwards, R. B. (Ed.). (1982). *Psychiatry and ethics: Insanity, rational autonomy, and mental health care.* Buffalo, NY: Prometheus Books.

Eliade, M. (1967). *Myths, dreams, and mysteries: The encounter between contemporary faiths and archaic realities.* New York: HarperCollins.

Elkin, I., Shea, M. T., Watkins, J. T., Imber, S. D., Sotsky, S. M., Collins, J. F., Glass, D. R., Pilkonis, P. A., Leber, W. R., Docherty, J. P., Fiester, S. J., & Parloff, M. B. (1989). NIMH Treatment of Depression Collaborative

Research Program: 1. General effectiveness of treatments. *Archives of General Psychiatry, 46*, 971–982.

Ellis, A. (1962). *Reason and emotion in psychotherapy*. New York: Citadel Press.

Ellis, A. (1973). *Humanistic psychotherapy: The rational-emotive approach*. New York: McGraw-Hill.

Ellis, A. (1983). *The case against religiosity*. New York: Institute for Rational-Emotive Therapy.

Ellul, J. (1965). *The technological society*. New York: Random House.

Erikson, E. H. (1968). *Identity, youth and crisis*. New York: Norton.

Eysenck, H. J. (1952). The effects of psychotherapy: An evaluation. *Journal of Consulting Psychology, 16*, 319–324.

Fancher, R. T. (1995). *Cultures of healing: Correcting the image of American mental health care*. New York: Freeman.

Flanagan, O. (1991). *Varieties of moral personality: Ethics and psychological realism*. Cambridge, MA: Harvard University Press.

Frank, J. D. (1961). *Persuasion and healing: A comparative study of psychotherapy*. Baltimore: Johns Hopkins University Press.

Frank, J. D. (1971). Therapeutic factors in psychotherapy. *American Journal of Psychotherapy, 25*, 350–361.

Frank, J. D. (1973). *Persuasion and healing: A comparative study of psychotherapy* (2nd ed.). Baltimore: Johns Hopkins University Press.

Frank, J. D., & Frank, J. B. (1991). *Persuasion and healing: A comparative study of psychotherapy* (3rd ed.). Baltimore: Johns Hopkins University Press.

Frankfurt, H. (1971). Freedom of the will and the concept of a person. *Journal of Philosophy, 67*, 5–20.

Freud, S. (1961a). *Civilization and its discontents* (J. Strachey, Trans.). New York: W. W. Norton. (Original work published 1930)

Freud, S. (1961b). The future of an illusion. In J. Strachey (Ed. and Trans.), *The standard edition of the complete psychological works of Sigmund Freud* (Vol. 21). London: Hogarth Press. (Original work published 1928)

Freud, S. (1961c). The question of lay analysis. In J. Strachey (Ed. and Trans.), *The standard edition of the complete psychological works of Sigmund Freud* (Vol. 20). London: Hogarth Press. (Original work published 1926)

Friedman, M. (1978). *To deny our nothingness: Contemporary images of man*. Chicago: University of Chicago Press.

Gadamer, H. G. (1975a). *Truth and method* (G. Burden & J. Cumming, Trans.). New York: Seabury Press.

Gadamer, H. G. (1975b). Hermeneutics and social science. *Cultural Hermeneutics, 2*, 307–316.

Gara, M. A., & Rosenberg, S. (1979). The identification of supersets and subsets in free-response vocabulary. *Journal of Personality and Social Psychology, 37*, 2161–2170.

Gardner, H. (1983). *Frames of mind: The theory of multiple intelligences*. New York: Basic Books.

Gartner, J., Larson, D. B., & Allen, G. D. (1991). Religious commitment and mental health: A review of the empirical literature. *Journal of Psychology and Theology, 19,* 6–25.

Geha, R. E. (1993). Transferred fictions. *Psychoanalytic Dialogues, 3,* 209–243.

Gehlen, A. (1980). *Man in the age of technology.* New York: Columbia University Press.

Gergen, K. J., & Kaye, J. (1992). Beyond narrative in the negotiation of therapeutic meaning. In S. McNamee & K. J. Gergen (Eds.), *Therapy as social construction* (pp. 166–185). Thousand Oaks, CA: Sage.

Giddens, A. (1991). *Modernity and self-identity: Self and society in the late modern age.* Stanford, CA: Stanford University Press.

Giorgi, A. (1970). *Psychology as a human science.* New York: HarperCollins.

Goffman, E. (1961). *Asylums.* Garden City, NY: Doubleday Anchor.

Goldfried, M. R. (1980). Toward a delineation of therapeutic change principles. *American Psychologist, 35,* 99–999.

Goleman, D. (1995). *Emotional intelligence.* New York: Bantam Books.

Gould, S. J. (1996). Creating the creators. *Discover, 17,* 42–54.

Gouldner, A. W. (1976). *The dialectic of ideology and technology.* New York: Seabury Press.

Grant, R. M. (1959). *Gnosticism and early Christianity.* New York: Columbia University Press.

Grünbaum, A. (1990). "Meaning" connections and causal connections in the human sciences: The poverty of hermeneutic philosophy. *Journal of the American Psychoanalytic Association, 38,* 559–578.

Guze, S. B. (1992). *Why psychiatry is a branch of medicine.* New York: Oxford University Press.

Habermas, J. (1971). *Knowledge and human interests* (J. Shapiro, Trans.). Boston: Beacon Press.

Heidegger, M. (1962). *Being and time* (J. Macquarrie & E. Robinson, Trans.). New York: HarperCollins. (Original work published 1927)

Heider, F. (1958). *The psychology of interpersonal relations.* New York: Wiley.

Heider, F., & Simmel, E. (1944). A study of apparent behavior. *American Journal of Psychology, 57,* 243–259.

Held, B. S. (1995). *Back to reality: A critique of postmodern theory in psychotherapy.* New York: Norton.

Hesse, M. (1980). *Revolutions and reconstructions in the philosophy of science.* Brighton, England: Harvester Press.

Hobbes, T. (1962). *Leviathan: Or the matter, forme and power of a commonwealth ecclesiasticall and civil* (M. Oakenshott, Ed.). New York: Macmillan. (Original work published 1651)

Horkheimer, M., & Adorno, T. (1972). *Dialectic of enlightenment.* New York: Seabury Press.

Horney, K. (1950). *Neurosis and human growth: The struggle toward self-realization.* New York: Norton.

Howard, K. I. (1995, August). *Outcome measures and consumer satisfaction—demonstrating value.* Paper presented at the annual meeting of the American Psychological Association, New York.

Hume, D. A. (1950). *Treatise of human nature* (Everyman ed.). New York: Dutton. (Original work published 1739)

Jacobson, N. S. (1995, August). *Psychotherapy is dead! Long live psychotherapy!* Paper presented at the annual meeting of the American Psychological Association, New York.

Jaeger, W. (1939). *Paideia: The ideals of Greek culture* (Vol. 1; G. Highet, Trans.). New York: Oxford University Press.

James, W. (1978). *Essays in philosophy.* Cambridge, MA: Harvard University Press. (Original work published 1878)

Jameson, F. (1981). *The political unconscious: Narrative as a socially symbolic act.* Ithaca, NY: Cornell University Press.

Janik, A., & Toulmin, S. (1973). *Wittgenstein's Vienna.* New York: Touchstone.

Jaspers, K. (1964). *The nature of psychotherapy: A critical appraisal* (J. Hoenig & M. W. Hamilton, Trans.). Chicago: University of Chicago Press.

Jung, C. G. (1933). *Modern man in search of a soul* (W. S. Dell & C. F. Baynes, Trans.). Orlando, FL: Harcourt Brace.

Jung, C. G. (1958). Psychology and religion: West and East. In R. F. C. Hull (Trans.), *Collected works* (Vol. 10). New York: Pantheon Books.

Kane, R. (1994). *Through the moral maze: Searching for absolute values in a pluralistic world.* New York: Paragon House.

Kazdin, A. E. (1978). *History of behavior modification: Experimental foundations of contemporary research.* Baltimore: University Park Press.

Kegan, R. (1982). *The evolving self: Problems and processes in human development.* Cambridge, MA: Harvard University Press.

Kelly, G. A. (1955). *The psychology of personal constructs.* New York: Norton.

Kelly, T. A. (1990). The role of values in psychotherapy: A critical review of process and outcome effects. *Clinical Psychology Review, 10,* 171–186.

Kierkegaard, S. (1959). *Either/Or* (Vol. 1; D. Swenson & L. Swenson, Trans.). Princeton, NJ: Princeton University Press. (Original work published 1843)

Kierkegaard, S. (1980). *The sickness unto death* (H. V. Hong & E. H. Hong, Trans.). Princeton, NJ: Princeton University Press. (Original work published 1849)

Kiev, A. (Ed.). (1964). *Magic, faith, and healing.* New York: Free Press.

Kim, M. P., & Rosenberg, S. (1980). Comparison of two structural models of implicit personality theory. *Journal of Personality and Social Psychology, 38,* 375–389.

Klein, G. S. (1976). *Psychoanalytic theory.* New York: International Universities Press.

Kuhn, T. S. (1970). *The structure of scientific revolutions* (2nd ed.). Chicago: University of Chicago Press.

Lakin, M. (1988). *Ethical issues in the psychotherapies*. New York: Oxford University Press.

Lambert, M. J., & Bergin, A. E. (1994). The effectiveness of psychotherapy. In A. E. Bergin & S. L. Garfield (Eds.), *Handbook of psychotherapy and behavior change* (4th ed.) (pp. 143–189). New York: Wiley.

Lasch, C. (1977). *Haven in a heartless world: The family besieged*. New York: Basic Books.

Lasch, C. (1978). *The culture of narcissism: American life in an age of diminishing expectations*. New York: Norton.

Laudan, L. (1984). *Science and values: The aims of science and their role in scientific debate*. Berkeley: University of California Press.

Lazarus, A. A. (1981). *The practice of multimodal therapy: Systematic, comprehensive, and effective psychotherapy*. New York: McGraw-Hill.

Lazarus, A. A. (1995). Different types of eclecticism and integration: Let's be aware of the dangers. *Journal of Psychotherapy Integration, 5*, 27–39.

Lazarus, R. S. (1991). *Emotion and adaptation*. New York: Oxford University Press.

Lee, A. M. (1954). Social pressures and the values of psychologists. *American Psychologist, 9*, 516–522.

Lerner, M. (1991). *Surplus powerlessness: The psychodynamics of everyday life—and the psychology of individual and social transformation*. Atlantic Highlands, NJ: Humanities Press International.

Leventhal, H. (1979). A perceptual-motor processing model of emotion. In P. Pliner, K. Blankstein, & I. M. Spigel (Eds.), *Advances in the study of communication and affect: Perception of emotion in self and others* (Vol. 5, pp. 1–46). New York: Plenum Press.

Levi-Strauss, C. (1963). *Structural anthropology*. New York: Basic Books.

Levitsky, A., & Perls, F. S. (1970). The rules and games of Gestalt therapy. In J. Fagan & I. L. Shepherd (Eds.), *Gestalt therapy now: Theory, techniques, applications* (pp. 140–149). New York: HarperCollins.

Levy, M. (1972). *Modernization: Latecomers and survivors*. New York: Basic Books.

Lewis, M. (1993). Self-conscious emotions: Embarrassment, pride, shame, and guilt. In M. Lewis & J. M. Haviland (Eds.), *Handbook of emotions* (pp. 563–573). New York: Guilford Press.

Lilienfeld, S. O., & Marino, L. (1995). Mental disorder as a Roschian concept: A critique of Wakefield's "harmful dysfunction" analysis. *Journal of Abnormal Psychology, 104*, 411–420.

Lipsey, M. W., & Wilson, D. B. (1993). The efficacy of psychological, educational, and behavioral treatment: Confirmation from meta-analysis. *American Psychologist, 48*, 1181–1209.

London, M. (1995). *Self and interpersonal insight: How people gain understanding of themselves and others in organizations*. New York: Oxford University Press.

London, P. (1964). *Modes and morals of psychotherapy*. New York: Holt, Rinehart and Winston.

Lowe, C. M. (1959). Value orientations: An ethical dilemma. *American Psychologist, 14*, 687–693.

Lyotard, J.-F. (1984). The *postmodern condition: A report on knowledge* (G. Bennington & B. Massumi, Trans.). Minneapolis: University of Minnesota Press.

MacIntyre, A. (1981). *After virtue*. South Bend, IN: University of Notre Dame Press.

Magee, B. (1982). *Men of ideas: Some creators of contemporary philosophy*. New York: Oxford University Press.

Mahoney, M. J. (1980). Psychotherapy and the structure of personal revolutions. In M. J. Mahoney (Ed.), *Psychotherapy process: Current issues and future directions* (pp. 157–180). New York: Plenum.

Makkreel, R. A. (1975). *Dilthey: Philosopher of the human studies*. Princeton, NJ: Princeton University Press.

Mannheim, K. (1960). *Ideology and utopia*. London: Routledge. (Original work published 1929)

Margolis, J. (1966). *Psychotherapy and morality*. New York: Random House.

Maslow, A. H. (1968). *Toward a psychology of being* (2nd ed.). New York: Van Nostrand Reinhold.

McAdams, D. P. (1996). Personality, modernity, and the storied self: A contemporary framework for studying persons. *Psychological Inquiry, 7*, 295–321.

McNeill, J. T. (1951). *A history of the cure of souls*. New York: HarperCollins.

Mead, G. H. (1934). *Mind, self and society*. Chicago: University of Chicago Press.

Meehl, P. M. (1997). Credentialed persons, credentialed knowledge. *Clinical Psychology: Science and Practice, 4*, 91–98.

Merton, R. (1973). *The sociology of science*. Chicago: University of Chicago Press.

Messer, S. B. (1986). Behavioral and psychoanalytic perspectives at therapeutic choice points. *American Psychologist, 41*, 1261–1272.

Messer, S. B., & Winokur, M. (1980). Some limits to the integration of psychoanalytic and behavior therapy. *American Psychologist, 35*, 818–827.

Michotte, A. E. (1963). *The perception of causality* (T. R. Miles & E. Miles, Trans.). London: Methuen. (Original work published 1946)

Mill, J. S. (1973). System of logic: Ratiocinative and inductive. In J. M. Robson (Ed.), *The collected works of John Stuart Mill* (Vols. 7 and 8). Toronto: University of Toronto Press. (Original work published 1843)

Mink, L. O. (1981). Everyman his or her own annalist. In W. J. T. Mitchell (Ed.), *On narrative* (pp. 233–239). Chicago: University of Chicago Press.

Mischel, W. (1968). *Personality and assessment*. New York: Wiley.

Mischel, W. (1973). Toward a cognitive social learning reconceptualization of personality. *Psychological Review, 80*, 252–283.

Moore, G. E. (1966). *Principia ethica*. Cambridge: Cambridge University Press. (Original work published 1903)

Murphy, G. (1955). The cultural context of guidance. *Personnel and Guidance Journal, 34*, 4–9.

Murray, E. J. (1956). A content-analysis method for studying psychotherapy. *Psychological Monographs, 70*(13, Whole No. 420).

Nagel, E. (1961). *The structure of science: Problems in the logic of scientific explanation*. Orlando, FL: Harcourt Brace.

Nagel, T. (1994, May 12). Freud's permanent revolution. *New York Review of Books*, pp. 34–38.

Neimeyer, R. A. (1993). An appraisal of constructivist psychotherapies. *Journal of Consulting and Clinical Psychology, 61*, 221–234.

Neisser, U. (1988). Five kinds of self-knowledge. *Philosophical Psychology, 1*, 35–39.

Nelson, B. (1975). Perspectives on the therapeutic in the context of contemporary sociology: A dialogue between Benjamin Nelson and Dennis Wong. In R. Boyers (Ed.), *Psychological man* (pp. 143–178). New York: HarperCollins.

Nelson, B. (1981). *On the roads to modernity: Conscience, science and civilizations* (T. E. Huff, Ed.). Totowa, NJ: Rowman and Littlefield.

Nisbet, R. (1967). *The sociological tradition*. New York: Basic Books.

Nisbet, R. (1975). *Twilight of authority*. New York: Oxford University Press.

Nisbet, R. (1976). *Sociology as an art form*. London: Oxford University Press.

Nisbett, R. E., & Wilson, T. D. (1977). Telling more than we can know: Verbal reports on mental processes. *Psychological Review, 84*, 231–259.

North, H. (1966). *Sophrosnye, self-knowledge and self-restraint in Greek literature*. Ithaca, NY: Cornell University Press.

Nussbaum, M. C. (1994). *The therapy of desire: Theory and practice in Hellenistic ethics*. Princeton, NJ: Princeton University Press.

Omer, H., & Strenger, C. (1992). The pluralist revolution: From one true meaning to an infinity of constructed ones. *Psychotherapy, 29*, 253–261.

Osgood, C. E., Suci, G. J., & Tannenbaum, P. H. (1957). *The measurement of meaning*. Urbana: University of Illinois Press.

Pagels, E. (1979). *The gnostic gospels*. New York: Vintage Books.

Palmer, R. E. (1969). *Hermeneutics: Interpretation theory in Schleiermacher, Dilthey, Heidegger and Gadamer*. Evanston, IL: Northwestern University Press.

Parry, A., & Doan, R. E. (1994). *Story revisions: Narrative therapy in the postmodern word*. New York: Guilford Press.

Parsons, T. (1977). *The evolution of societies*. Upper Saddle River, NJ: Prentice-Hall.

Peabody, D. (1967). Trait inferences: Evaluative and descriptive aspects. *Journal of Personality and Social Psychology Monographs, 7*(Whole No. 644).

Perls, F. S. (1969). *Gestalt therapy verbatim*. Lafayette, CA: Real People Press.

Polanyi, K. (1957). *The great transformation*. Boston: Beacon Press.

Polanyi, M. (1958). *Personal knowledge: Toward a post-critical philosophy.* Chicago: University of Chicago Press.

Polkinghorne, D. E. (1988). *Narrative knowing and the human sciences.* Albany: State University of New York Press.

Putnam, H. (1981). *Reason, truth and history.* Cambridge: Cambridge University Press.

Randall, J. H. (1926). *The making of the modern mind: A survey of the intellectual background of the present age.* Boston: Houghton Mifflin.

Ricoeur, P. (1970). *Freud and philosophy: An essay on interpretation* (D. Savage, Trans.). New Haven, CT: Yale University Press.

Ricoeur, P. (1981). *Hermeneutics and the human sciences: Essays on language, action and interpretation* (J. B. Thompson, Ed. and Trans.). Cambridge: Cambridge University Press.

Rieff, P. (1959). *Freud: The mind of the moralist.* Chicago: University of Chicago Press.

Rieff, P. (1966). *The triumph of the therapeutic: Uses of faith after Freud.* New York: HarperCollins.

Rogers, C. R. (1961). *On becoming a person.* Boston: Houghton Mifflin.

Rogers, C. R. (1964). Toward a science of the person. In T. W. Wann (Ed.), *Behaviorism and phenomenology: Contrasting bases for modern psychology* (pp. 109–140). Chicago: The University of Chicago Press.

Rogers, C. R. (1980). *A way of being.* Boston: Houghton Mifflin.

Rorty, R. (1991). *Objectivity, relativism, and truth: Philosophical papers* (Vol. 1). Cambridge: Cambridge University Press.

Rosch, E. R. (1973). Natural categories. *Cognitive Psychology, 4,* 328–350.

Rousseau, J.-J. (1911). *Emile* (B. Foxley, Trans.). London: Dent. (Original work published 1762)

Rozin, P., Haidt, J., McCauley, C. R. (1993). Disgust. In M. Lewis & J. M. Haviland (Eds.), *Handbook of emotions* (pp. 575–594). New York: Guilford Press.

Sabini, J., & Silver, M. (1982). *Moralities of everyday life.* Oxford: Oxford University Press.

Sagan, C. (1995). *The demon-haunted world: Science as a candle in the dark.* New York: Random House.

Salovey, P., & Mayer, J. D. (1990). Emotional intelligence. *Imagination, Cognition, and Personality, 9,* 185–211.

Sartre, J. (1949). *Existentialism is a humanism* (P. Mairet, Trans.). New York: Philosophical Library. (Original work published 1946)

Sartre, J. (1956). *Being and nothingness* (H. Barnes, Trans.). New York: Philosophical Library.

Sass, L. A., & Woolfolk, R. L. (1988). Truth: Narrative and historical. *Journal of the American Psychoanalytic Association, 36,* 429–454.

Schafer, R. (1978). *Language and insight.* New Haven, CT: Yale University Press.

Schafer, R. (1981). *Narrative actions in psychoanalysis.* Worcester, MA: Clark University Press.

Schafer, R. (1983). *The analytic attitude.* New York: Basic Books.

Schleiermacher, F. D. E. (1985). Foundations: General theory and art of interpretation (J. Duke & J. Forstman, Trans.). In K. Mueller-Vollmer (Ed.), *The hermeneutics reader* (pp. 72–97). New York: Continuum. (Original work published 1819)

Schutz, A. (1962). On multiple realities. In *Collected papers* (Vol. 1, pp. 209–259). The Hague: Nijhoff.

Searle, J. R. (1984). *Minds, brains and science.* Cambridge, MA: Harvard University Press.

Searle, J. R. (1995). *The construction of social reality.* New York: Free Press.

Sedgwick, P. (1982). *Psycho politics.* New York: HarperCollins.

Seligman, M. E. P. (1994). *What you can change and what you can't: The complete guide to successful self-improvement.* New York: Knopf.

Seligman, M. E. P. (1995). The effectiveness of psychotherapy: The Consumer Reports study. *American Psychologist, 50,* 965–974.

Sennett, R. (1977). *The fall of public man.* Cambridge: Cambridge University Press.

Sherman, C. (1993). Behind closed doors: Therapist-client sex. *Psychology Today, 26,* 64–72.

Sherwood, M. (1969). *The logic of explanation in psychoanalysis.* New York: Academic Press.

Shiner, L. E. (1967). The concept of secularization in empirical research. *Journal for the Scientific Study of Religion, 6,* 207–220.

Sileo, C. (1995, June 12). Unearthed memories lose ground in court. *Insight on the News,* pp. 14–15.

Skinner, B. F. (1983). Intellectual self-management in old age. *American Psychologist, 38,* 239–244.

Sloane, R. B., Staples, F. R., Cristol, A. H., Yorkston, N. J., & Whipple, K. (1975). *Psychotherapy versus behavior therapy.* Cambridge, MA: Harvard University Press.

Smith, M. L., Glass, G. V., & Miller, T. L. (1980). *The benefits of psychotherapy.* Baltimore: Johns Hopkins University Press.

Snow, C. P. (1970). *The two cultures and a second look.* Cambridge: Cambridge University Press.

Spence, D. (1982). *Narrative truth and historical truth.* New York: Norton.

Spulber, N. (1995). *The American economy: The struggle for supremacy in the 21st century.* New York: Cambridge University Press.

Steele, R. S. (1979). Psychoanalysis and hermeneutics. *International Review of Psychoanalysis, 6,* 389–411.

Steiner, R. (1995). Hermeneutics or Hermes-mess. *International Journal of Psychoanalysis, 76,* 435–445.

Sternberg, R. J., Wagner, R. K., Williams, W. M., & Horvath, J. A. (1995). Testing common sense. *American Psychologist, 50,* 912–927.

Strupp, H. H., & Hadley, S. W. (1979). Specific versus non-specific factors in psychotherapy: A controlled study of outcome. *Archives of General Psychiatry, 36,* 1125–1136.

Sue, D. W., & Sue, S. (1990). *Counseling the culturally different.* New York: Wiley.

Szasz, T. S. (1978). *The myth of psychotherapy.* Garden City, NY: Doubleday Anchor.

Szasz, T. S. (1983). *Thomas Szasz: Primary values and major contentions* (R. E. Vatz & L. S. Weinberg, Eds.). Buffalo: Prometheus Books.

Taylor, C. (1975). *Hegel.* Cambridge: Cambridge University Press.

Taylor, C. (1985). *Human agency and language: Philosophical papers I.* Cambridge: Cambridge University Press.

Taylor, C. (1988). The moral topography of the self. In S. B. Messer, L. A. Sass, & R. L. Woolfolk (Eds.), *Hermeneutics and psychological theory: Interpretive perspectives on personality, psychotherapy, and psychopathology* (pp. 289–320). New Brunswick, NJ: Rutgers University Press.

Taylor, C. (1989). *Sources of the self: The making of the modern identity.* Cambridge, MA: Harvard University Press.

Tocqueville, A. de. (1966). *Democracy in America* (J. P. Mayer, Ed.; G. Lawrence, Trans.). New York: HarperCollins. (Original work published 1848)

Toffler, A. (1980). *The third wave.* New York: Morrow.

Tooby, J., & Cosmides, L. (1990). The past explains the present: Emotional adaptation and the structure of ancestral environments. *Ethology and Sociobiology, 11,* 375–424.

Toulmin, S. (1954). The logical status of psycho-analysis. In M. MacDonald (Ed.), *Philosophy and analysis* (pp. 132–139). New York: Philosophical Library.

Trilling, L. (1971). *Sincerity and authenticity.* Cambridge, MA: Harvard University Press.

Truax, C. B. (1966). Reinforcement and nonreinforcement in Rogerian psychotherapy. *Journal of Abnormal Psychology, 71,* 1–9.

Tugendhat, E. (1986). *Self-consciousness and self-determination* (P. Stern, Trans.). Cambridge, MA: MIT Press.

Ullmann, L. P., & Krasner, L. (1969). *A psychological approach to abnormal behavior.* Upper Saddle River, NJ: Prentice-Hall.

VandenBos, G. R. (1996). Outcome assessment of psychotherapy. *American Psychologist, 51,* 1005–1006.

Veatch, R. M. (1973). The medical model: Its nature and problems. *Hastings Center Studies, 1,* 59–76.

Veroff, J., Kulka, R. A., & Douvan, E. (1981). *Mental health in America: Patterns of help-seeking from 1957 to 1976.* New York: Basic Books.

Vitz, P. C. (1977). *Psychology as religion: The cult of self-worship.* Grand Rapids, MI: Eerdmans.

Vitz, P. C. (1985). The dilemma of narcissism. *Journal of Social and Clinical Psychology, 3*, 9–14.

Wagner, R. K., & Sternberg, R. J. (1986). Tacit knowledge and intelligence in the everyday world. In R. J. Sternberg and R. K. Wagner (Eds.), *Practical intelligence: Nature and origins of competence in the everyday world* (pp. 51–83). Cambridge: Cambridge University Press.

Wakefield, J. C. (1992). The concept of mental disorder: On the boundary between biological facts and social values. *American Psychologist, 47*, 373–388.

Wakefield, J. C. (1993). Limits of operationalization: A critique of Spitzer and Endicott's (1978) proposed operational criteria for mental disorder. *Journal of Abnormal Psychology, 102*, 160–172.

Wallach, M. A., & Wallach, L. (1983). *Psychology's sanction for selfishness: The error of egoism in theory and therapy.* New York: Freeman.

Watson, D., & Clark, L. A. (1984). Negative affectivity: The disposition to experience aversive emotional states. *Psychological Bulletin, 96*, 465–490.

Weber, M. (1946). *From Max Weber* (H. H. Gerth & C. W. Mills, Eds. and Trans.). New York: Oxford University Press.

Weber, M. (1978). [Letter to Edgar Jaffé written in 1907]. In W. G. Runciman (Ed.), *Max Weber: Selections in translation* (E. Matthews, Trans., pp. 383–388). Cambridge: Cambridge University Press.

Wellmer, A. (1991). *The persistence of modernity: Essays on aesthetics, ethics, and postmodernism.* Cambridge, MA: MIT Press.

Wender, P. H., & Klein, D. F. (1981). *Mind, mood, and medicine: A guide to the new biological psychiatry.* New York: Farrar, Straus & Giroux.

White, H. (1973). *Metahistory: The historical imagination in nineteenth-century Europe.* Baltimore: Johns Hopkins University Press.

White, M., & Epston, D. (1990). *Narrative means to therapeutic ends.* New York: Norton.

Williams, B. (1995). *Making sense of humanity and other philosophical papers.* Cambridge: Cambridge University Press.

Wilson, G. T. (1995). Manual-based treatments: The clinical application of research findings. *Behaviour Research and Therapy, 34*, 295–314.

Wilson, G. T., & O'Leary, K. D. (1980). *Principles of behavior therapy.* Engelwood Cliffs, NJ: Prentice-Hall.

Winch, P. (1958). *The idea of a social science and its relation to philosophy.* London: Routledge.

Winner, L. (1977). *Autonomous technology: Technics-out-of-control as a theme in political thought.* Cambridge, MA: MIT Press.

Wittgenstein, L. (1953). *Philosophical investigations* (G. E. M. Ambscome, Trans.). London: Basil Blackwell.

Wolin, R. (Ed.). (1991). *The Heidegger controversy: A critical reader.* New York: Columbia University Press.

Wollheim, R. (1993). *The mind and its depths*. Cambridge: Harvard University Press.

Woolfolk, A. E., & Woolfolk, R. L., & Wilson, G. T. (1977). A rose by any other name: Labeling bias and attitudes toward behavior modification. *Journal of Consulting and Clinical Psychology, 45*, 184–191.

Woolfolk, R. L., Novalany, J., Gara, M. A., Allen, L. A., & Polino, M. (1995). Self-complexity, self-evaluation, and depression: An examination of form and content within the self-schema. *Journal of Personality and Social Psychology, 68*, 1108–1120.

Woolfolk, R. L., & Richardson, F. C. (1984). Behavior therapy and the ideology of modernity. *American Psychologist, 39*, 777–786.

Woolfolk, R. L., & Sass, L. A. (1988). Behaviorism and existentialism revisited. *Journal of Humanistic Psychology, 28*, 108–119.

Woolfolk, R. L., Sass, L. A., & Messer, S. M. (1988). Introduction to hermeneutics. In S. M. Messer, L. A. Sass, & R. L. Woolfolk (Eds.), *Hermeneutics and psychological theory* (pp. 2–26). New Brunswick, NJ: Rutgers University Press.

Zajonc, R. B. (1980). Cognition and social cognition: A historical perspective. In L. Festinger (Ed.), *Retrospections on social psychology* (pp. 180–204). Oxford: Oxford University Press.

Zajonc, R. B. (1984). On the primacy of affect. In K. S. Scherer & P. Ekman (Eds.), *Approaches to emotion* (pp. 259–270). Hillsdale, NJ: Erlbaum.

The Author

ROBERT L. WOOLFOLK is currently professor of psychology at Rutgers University. He also has served on the faculties of Princeton University, the University of Texas at Austin, and the Robert Wood Johnson Medical School. Woolfolk has functioned both as a scientist and a clinician. He is the author of numerous papers reporting empirical research on the treatment and diagnosis of anxiety and depression. His most recent research involves determining the structure of social cognition in psychopathological states. He also has written widely on the philosophical and sociocultural underpinnings of psychotherapy. A licensed clinical psychologist, Woolfolk has been a practicing psychotherapist and trainer of clinicians for twenty-five years. He was formerly director of clinical training at Rutgers. Woolfolk is the coeditor of *Principles and Practice of Stress Management* and of *Hermeneutics and Psychological Theory*. He coauthored *Stress, Sanity, and Survival*.

Name Index

A

Adler, A., 29
Adorno, T., 77–78
Albert, E. A., 60
Allen, G. D., 50
Allen, L. A., 107
Apollo, 46, 59, 63
Aristarchus of Samos, 101
Aristotle, 59, 75, 117, 120–121, 122, 123, 137, 141, 144
Augustine, 60, 61
Ayer, A. J., 53

B

Bandura, A., 44, 136–137, 146
Bargh, J. A., 54
Barlow, D. H., 125
Barthes, R., 99
Baumeister, R. F., 57
Beck, A. T., 17, 127
Bell, D., 9
Bellah, R. N., 24, 25, 26, 27, 34, 128
Bem, D. J., 136–137
Bergan, J., 48
Berger, B., 12
Berger, P. L., 12, 19, 46
Bergin, A. E., 17, 34, 47–50, 145
Beutler, L. E., 48, 133, 145
Booth, J. W., 70
Bourdieu, P., 23, 111, 112–113
Brinton, C., 14
Bubner, R., 110
Buss, D. M., 119
Butt, M. M., 28
Byron, G. G., 62

C

Campbell, J., 15
Campbell, T. W., 146
Camus, A., 12
Carr, D., 98
Christensen, A., 145
Clark, L. A., 143
Comte, A., 68
Conrad, P., 140
Copernicus, N., 101
Copi, I. M., 143
Cosmides, L., 119
Craske, M. G., 125
Crews, F., 130
Cristol, A. H., 144
Crites, S., 98
Cromwell, O., 141
Cushman, P., 18, 35
Cutter, F., 1

D

Danto, A. C., 70, 99, 100–101
Davis, K., 128
Dawes, R. M., 30, 145
Denise, T. C., 60
Descartes, R., 14, 72
Dewey, J., 54, 115
Dicks, H. V., 17
Dihle, A., 59
Dilthey, W., 5, 67–72, 79, 84, 131, 135, 136, 141, 142
Dionysus, 46, 63
Doan, R. E., 89
Doherty, W. J., 28
Douvan, E., 30
Dreyfus, H. L., 111, 114
Droysen, J. G., 69

Subject Index

A

Alcoholics Anonymous, 1
American Psychiatric Association, 131
American Psychological Association, 127
Anger, concept of, 117, 144
Application, and practical knowledge,
122–126
Ausdruck, and hermeneutics, 70–71

B

Background, and practical knowledge,
111–115, 118, 126
Behavior therapy, critique of, 42–47
Belittlement, forms of, 144
Biology, and psychiatry, 35–42
*Brown v. Board of Education of Topeka,
Kansas*, 123

C

Capitalism, and secularization, 25
Causal powers, and self-understanding,
104–106
Children, sexual abuse of, 129–130,
132–133, 146
Cognition: and emotions, 96–97,
143–144; interests of, 78–80
Cognitive-behavior therapy, applying,
124–125
Cognitive social learning theory, 44
Communitarians, and modernity, 24–26,
28
Conditioning theory, and behavior ther-
apy, 43–45
Constructivism, and hermeneutics,
134–136
Cosmologies, premodern, 12, 19

Critical Theory, and hermeneutics,
77–78, 80
Culture: of narcissism, 23–24; therapeutic, 22
Cure of souls: concept of, 139; and min-
istry, 16

D

Democracy, and modernity, 26–29
Diagnostic and Statistical Manual (DSM),
44, 51, 131
Directive structures concept, 19
Disgust, concept of, 117

E

Efficacy, of psychotherapy, 33–34,
128–130, 144–146
Emotions: and behavior therapy, 46–47;
and cognition, 96–97, 143–144; and
humanism, 63–64; intelligence for,
118–120; and values, 116–120
Engagement, and evaluation, in practical
knowledge, 116–120
Enlightenment: and humanism, 62; and
modernity, 11, 13
Epicureans, and humanism, 59–60
Episteme, and *techne*, 120–121
Erlebuis, and hermeneutics, 69, 71
Ethics: and modernity, 17–21; and psy-
chotherapy, 141
Evaluation: and engagement, 116–120;
second-order, 107
Everydayness, and practical knowledge,
110–111
Evolution: and emotional intelligence,
119; science and values in, 51–53
Exaptations concept, 52